CHAPTER 1

P9-CAV-571

GETTING STARTED

GETTING STARTED

INTRODUCTION

Welcome to FIRAXIS Games™ second offering, *Sid Meier's Alpha Centauri™*. As with all games from FIRAXIS, fun and imagination rule, and we have tried to make a very complex topic accessible and interesting.

It is an ambitious game, addressing some very fundamental issues facing mankind as we approach the new millennium. What sort of technologies can we expect to deal with within the next couple of centuries? How will we use these technologies — for good or for evil? In fact, what ideologies will be paramount in the next millennium, and do these ideologies imply new and differing definitions for "good" and "evil"? What is the ultimate goal for humanity?

THE STORY

Soon after the new millenium begins, humankind's oldest enemies — war, famine and disease — are winning the battle on planet Earth. The United Nations decides to attempt the mission that has been the dream of countless science fiction writers and fans for generations: the colonization of a New World, before it is too late. The establishment of a new outpost for mankind as an alternative to the decaying situation on our mother planet seems to be the last and best hope for the continued existence of mankind.

Code named "Unity," the plan is simple. Send enough men, women and supplies to the earthlike planet, Chiron, orbiting the primary star in the Alpha Centauri system. Give them the seeds for planting a new society — technology, knowledge, and experts of every kind. Insure that the mission, U.N. sponsored, stays on track by carefully monitoring its progress from Earth. Then, when the time is right, and if the need still exists, begin shuttling others to the New World at Alpha Centauri.

But space travel is a difficult undertaking, even now. It is hard to reach our own moon. Even if we had the capacity to make it to a distant planet, will we be able to bring the travelers back? Once firmly established on a distant world, will we be able to cooperate with one another there long enough to establish a new society that can attain the same levels and quality of life that we have achieved here after almost 5000 years of civilization? But the deteriorating conditions on Earth leave us little choice.

From the beginning, there are problems aboard the U.N. Starship *Unity*. An unexpected reactor malfunction damages the ship, waking the travelers early from cryo-sleep. It soon is evident that the accident has damaged the communications equipment and contact with Earth is lost, and cannot be re-established. The leadership of the mission is faced with the prospect of going it alone and soon begin to argue obstinately about the best way to proceed.

The game begins when the Unity Mission reaches Chiron. But, by this time, the mission has fallen into chaos. The most powerful leaders on board have built ideological factions and surrounded themselves with dedicated followers. It is clear that each faction has established its own agenda for the future of mankind and is desperately serious about carrying it through.

GOOD LUCK

We hope you will find a multitude of ways to solve the problems the *Unity* travelers face. There are nearly unlimited options and you can experiment relentlessly as you explore, discover, build and conquer. Please feel free to contact us to pass on criticism or praise, or just your point of view, at WWW.FIRAXIS.COM. Have fun and Good Luck. — FIRAXIS Games

USING THE MANUAL

If this is the very first time you've ever played *Sid Meier's Alpha Centauri* or any game like it, we recommend you do *not* sit down and read this book cover-to-cover before you start playing!

Instead, we strongly suggest you put down this book, start up the game, and play through the tutorial scenario provided. Also, check out the five "tours" provided in the game's Help menu. These two resources are the easiest (and most fun) way to learn the basics of the game.

Tours. To get to the tours, start the game and select any options which look interesting (you'll find out exactly what they do a little later) or just hit QUICK START. When the game loads for the first time, you will be automatically walked through several tours that show you the fundamentals of the game. To get back to the tours after the first game, 🖰 (left-click) on the MENU tab on the left side of the screen, then 🖰 on HELP. The tours are at the bottom of the Help menu.

Tutorial Scenarios. To access the tutorial scenarios, start the game and select SCENARIO from the Main menu. When the Scenario menu appears, select PLAY SCENARIO. Open the folder 1EXPLORE and select the "Explore.sc" file. Upon successful completion of the "Explore" scenario, move on to the 2BUILD folder, and then to the 3CONQUER folder. When played in succession, these tutorials can help teach the *Sid Meier's Alpha Centauri* basics in a fun and intuitive way. To access a list of scenario objectives and how to achieve them, 🖰 on the MENU tab on the left side of the screen, then 🖰 on the HQ menu, and select REVIEW SCENARIO OBJECTIVES.

4

Once you know the basics, this manual is provided to help you discover the many subtleties and details of *Sid Meier's Alpha Centauri*. We hope you'll be returning to these pages often while playing, to discover the exact purpose behind a game option, or the meaning of a term. Who knows? Maybe after you've been playing *Sid Meier's Alpha Centauri* for awhile, you'll come back and read this book cover-to-cover, just to make sure you're not missing anything.

In addition to this manual, you will find the following materials, also included with your game, extremely useful:

- **Install Guide.** Installation, trouble shooting and customer support.

- **Tech Tree Chart.** The technologies that you discover as you progress, and their interrelationships. This chart also contains information about the terrain, vehicles, and world of *Sid Meier's Alpha Centauri*.

This manual is divided into seven major sections:

- **Getting Started.** Loading and customizing your game.

- **Welcome to Alpha Centauri.** Movement, and the basic game interface.

- **Planet.** The ecology of the new world, and terraforming.

- **Colonizing Planet.** Building bases and expanding and defending your faction's territory.

- **Controlling Society.** The finer points of economics, diplomacy, research and Social Engineering.

- **Appendices,** listed below.

- A New Sun, **Planetography** and **Journey to Centauri,** giving background details on the world of *Sid Meier's Alpha Centauri.*

The appendices provide easy access to important information:

- **Notes and Tips.** Designer's notes, and some strategy tips.

- **Tables.** Quick reference charts to the technologies, units, facilities and Secret Projects available in the game.

- **Option Screens.** Quick reference listing of configurable options to customize gameplay.

- **Advanced Customization.** Advanced methods for customizing the game.

- **Index.** A complete listing of where to find details on all key topics in the game.

5

INSTALLATION

Installation, troubleshooting and customer support are all covered in the **Install Guide.**

GAME SETUP

Sid Meier's Alpha Centauri allows a wide range of player customization options both before and during play.

MAIN (STARTING) MENU

This is the first thing you see upon starting *Sid Meier's Alpha Centauri*.

You can quit the game from the Main menu with [Esc]. If you're not on the Main menu, [Esc] takes you back to your previous screen. On all menu screens, [Esc] takes you back one level.

START GAME

Starts a new game. This selection opens the Map Selection menu (see **Map Selection** menu, facing page).

QUICK START

This option drops you directly into a new game configured exactly like the last game you played (including faction choice). If you use Quick Start before playing any other games, it drops you into a world of average size, with all defaults on, playing the Gaian faction on the easiest difficulty level.

SCENARIO

Scenarios are specific challenges designed to test your playing skill to the maximum. The exceptions are the Tutorial Scenarios, specially designed to teach new players the basics.

LOAD GAME

Allows you to load a previously saved game. You can load both automatic saves (see **Automatic Saves, p. 30**) and named saves (see **Save Game, p. 29**).

This option opens your Saves directory.

MULTIPLAYER

Use this to set up a multiplayer game. See **Multiplayer**, in the **Install Guide**, for detailed instructions.

VIEW CREDITS

Reveals the game's creators.

EXIT GAME

This option quits the game and returns you to Windows®.

MAP SELECTION MENU

In this menu you decide what kind of new game you wish to start.

MAKE RANDOM MAP

Allows you to start a new game, making only a few basic choices— Size of Planet, Difficulty Level, Game Rules and Faction. (See **Customized Planets**, next page, for details of these options.)

MAKE RANDOM MAP

CUSTOMIZE RANDOM MAP

THE MAP OF PLANET

HUGE MAP OF PLANET

LOAD MAP FILE

CUSTOMIZE RANDOM MAP

Allows you to customize a number of parameters of your new world before you start play. See **Customized Planets**, next page, for details.

THE MAP OF PLANET

This map is the "official" map of Planet. It's always the same.

HUGE MAP OF PLANET

This is a large version of the map of Planet.

LOAD MAP FILE

This allows you to load a custom map that you've saved out as a map file.

CUSTOMIZED PLANETS

When you elect to play on a random or customized random map game, you're given a series of choices that allow you to shape the environment of your new world.

A fully customized planet allows you to control exactly what kind of game experience you want. If your primary interest is combat and tactics, choose a small planet with plentiful native life, giving you lots of opportunity to fight off native threats and other factions. If you're more interested in peaceful, long-term development, choose a huge planet and rare native life. If you want a difficult terraforming challenge, choose a mountainous, dry world, but if you want a more inviting environment for your people, choose rolling terrain and lots of rainfall. If you like building and managing a navy, go for extensive ocean coverage, or if you prefer to work on land, choose smaller oceans.

At any time in the customization process you can return to the Select Size of Planet menu by hitting (Esc).

SIZE

There are five options: **Tiny**, **Small**, **Standard**, **Large** and **Huge**. The bigger the world, the longer you'll probably play before encountering any of the other factions.

From this screen, you can also load any custom map files you may have saved. The **Load Map File** option opens your map file directory.

OCEAN COVERAGE

Allows you to select how much of the world is under water. The three options are **30-50%**, **50-70%**, and **70-90%**. The more ocean, the greater the necessity for a navy and the fewer opportunities to expand your faction on land.

EROSIVE FORCES

Allows you to choose between **Strong** (rolling and flat terrain), **Average** (hilly terrain), and **Weak** (rough, mountainous terrain). In general, flat terrain is easier to settle and terraform. Rougher surfaces are harder to terraform, but offer an abundance of mineral resources.

NATIVE LIFE FORMS

Allows you to select the frequency of Planet's native life-forms, notably mind worms (see **Fauna**, p. 40) and xenofungus (see **Flora**, p. 39). Choices are **Rare**, **Average** and **Abundant**. The fewer native life forms, the easier the going, particularly early in the game.

CLOUD COVER

The choices are **Sparse** (light rainfall), **Average**, and **Dense** (heavy rainfall). The more rainfall, the more nutrients available to feed and expand your bases.

DIFFICULTY

There are six levels of difficulty. The higher the difficulty, the smarter and more aggressive your opponents, and the tougher it is to establish and expand your faction. Difficulty levels, from easiest to hardest, are: **Citizen** (novice), **Specialist**, **Talent**, **Librarian**, **Thinker**, and **Transcend** (expert).

GAME RULES

These advanced gameplay options are described in detail under **Game Rules**, p. 197.

FACTION

There are seven factions of refugees from the disastrous destruction of the U.N. Starship *Unity*. This is where you select the one that you wish to lead.

- CUSTOM NAME allows you to change the name of the faction (if, for example, your faction simply *must* be the Cheeseheads). This option also allows you to customize the terms used to address and describe your faction in diplomatic interactions.

- HELP button displays a summary of the faction's character and its special abilities (and handicaps).

- LOAD lets you load a previously created faction configuration.

- OK accepts your choice and starts the game.

- CANCEL returns to the Main menu.

After you select a faction, you get a window that allows you to change the name and gender of your faction leader (for example, Norma of the Cheeseheads), if you wish, after which the game begins.

See **Factions**, facing page, for information about the seven factions themselves.

FACTIONS

The human factions of Planet are not divided by race, language or place of ancestral origin. Instead, each faction is guided by the vision of its leader. These visions, in turn, give each faction a unique set of advantages and disadvantages. By comparing the strengths of your faction to the parameters of a customized planet, you can either give yourself an edge against the other factions, or set yourself a unique challenge to overcome.

You're likely to find the game more enjoyable if you pick a faction you can empathize with (even if you don't necessarily agree with everything they profess).

GAIA'S STEPDAUGHTERS (LED BY LADY DEIRDRE SKYE)

The Gaians are determined not to repeat the environmental mistakes of old Earth. They seek to live at peace with Planet. They start out with the Centauri Ecology technology and advanced abilities to interact with the native life, including the ability to move freely through xenofungus squares and gather extra nutrients from fungus. Their empathy with Planet gives them the ability to place ravaging wild mind worms directly under their control. Their experience with recycling systems makes their bases more efficient, but their pacifist leanings undermine the abilities of their military units, and they resent police control in times of crisis. Because of negative environmental consequences, the Gaians can not make the "Free Market Economics" social choice (see **Society Window**, p. 136).

HUMAN HIVE (LED BY CHAIRMAN SHENG-JI YANG)

This faction is ruled under harsh collectivist/authoritarian principles. The good of the individual is totally subordinate to the state. They are isolationist, and militaristic. The Hive begins with the Doctrine: Loyalty technology. Their bases are built underground, giving them the equivalent of a pre-installed Perimeter Defense facility. Their population growth and industrial development are above average, but their economy tends to lag behind others. The Hive can not make the "Democratic" social choice (see **Society Window**, p. 136).

UNIVERSITY OF PLANET (LED BY ACADEMICIAN PROKHOR ZAKHAROV)

The University is completely dedicated to research and the free exchange of information. They are rumored to sometimes put the pursuit of knowledge ahead of ethics. They start the game with the Information Networks technology and one additional bonus technology. Each University base receives a free Network Node when founded. The University's research progresses quickly, but their open-access philosophy makes them susceptible to attacks by covert "Probe Teams," while their callous elitism can easily lead to unrest among the workers. The University can not make the "Fundamentalist" social choice (see **Society Window**, p. 136).

MORGAN INDUSTRIES (LED BY CEO NWABUDIKE MORGAN)

The Morganites are organized along corporate lines, and dedicated to laissez-faire capitalist economic principles. They start the game with 100 energy credits and the Industrial Base technology, and receive a bonus to all income from commerce between factions. Morganites have expensive tastes, making it difficult for them to support units in the field, and requiring them to build Hab Complex facilities before the population of any of their bases can exceed four citizens. The Morganites can not make the "Planned Economics" social choice (see **Society Window**, p. 136).

SPARTAN FEDERATION (LED BY COLONEL CORAZON SANTIAGO)

The Spartans are paramilitary survivalists. They believe in both a right and a duty to keep and bear arms. The Spartans start the game with the Doctrine: Mobility technology and a fast scout rover vehicle, and they do not have to pay extra to develop prototypes of new units. Morale of their units is exceptionally high, and their citizens accept strict police control as a necessity, but their extravagant military needs weigh down industrial operations. The Spartans can not make the "Wealth" social choice (See **Society Window**, p. 136).

THE LORD'S BELIEVERS (LED BY SISTER MIRIAM GODWINSON)

The Believers seek a life of prayer and religious worship. Because of the strength of their convictions, they get a bonus when attacking their enemies. They start the game with the Social Psych technology. The Believers are resistant to probe brainwashing, but their suspicion of secular science retards their research efforts, and their belief that Planet is their promised land sometimes interferes with their ecological sensitivity. The Believers can not make the "Knowledge" social choice (see **Society Window**, p. 136).

THE PEACEKEEPING FORCES (LED BY COMMISSIONER PRAVIN LAL)

The Peacekeepers exist to support the humanitarian principles of the United Nations of Earth, the organization that originally commissioned the *Unity* expedition to Alpha Centauri. They start the game with the Biogenetics technology. The idealism of this faction attracts an intellectual elite, but their society possesses a tendency towards bureaucratic inefficiency. Their bases can exceed normal population limits by 2. Due to his experience with parliamentary maneuvering, Lal's vote counts double when the Planetary Council is convened for election of a Planetary Governor or Supreme Leader. The Peacekeepers can not make the "Police State" social choice (see **Society Window**, p. 136).

CHAPTER 2

WELCOME TO ALPHA CENTAURI

WELCOME TO ALPHA CENTAURI

Your new home in the Alpha Centauri system is officially called *Chiron*, but most of the new inhabitants refer to it as *Planet*. In cosmic terms, Earth and Planet are two worlds similar enough to be considered practically identical. But for human beings, the product of millions of years of earth-specific evolution, Planet is a strange, alien and frightening place. Your first task, upon arrival on this new world, is figuring out the ground rules how the whole system of Planet works together, and how your faction can make itself profitably a part of that system.

GETTING STARTED

A whole new world is a big place, and *Sid Meier's Alpha Centauri* is a big game. The first settlers on Planet are awed by the infinite possibilities that stretch before them, and the first time you open the game, you might find yourself a bit over-awed by all the choices you have (particularly if you've never played any similar simulations before). This section is a quick guide to what you can expect when you first start to play, and some of the basic and necessary actions you need to take to get yourself established. All the concepts and actions mentioned below are covered in much greater detail later in this book.

FOLLOWING PLANETFALL

When your faction first makes planetfall, you always have at least one mobile unit ready for action. Send this unit out to explore the immediate vicinity of your base (you can move your unit with the eight arrow keys on the numeric keypad: just press the key corresponding to the direction you want to go). Try to explore at least five or six squares out from the base in all directions, then pick a direction and head out, or find a coastline and follow it. You're look-ing for inviting places to establish new bases (remember, green is good – look for green squares near rivers or coastlines), and for the supply pods scattered by the *Unity* just before its destruction (but be careful—the *Unity* pods can contain valuable gifts, but they can also unleash danger). Watch out for mind worm boils—the dangerous native life-forms of Planet. Be prepared to fight or run when you see mind worms (you can attack by attempting to move into their square). Ultimately, you'll want to make contact with the units or bases of the other human factions.

RESEARCHING TECHNOLOGY

New technologies drive your survival and expansion on Planet, giving you access to new weapons, base facilities, and Secret Projects. As soon as your first base is established, your faction immediately begins scientific research. You don't have to do anything to start researching, it just happens. Every few turns your scientists announce a new breakthrough, and ask you to set priorities to guide your next research effort. For more information on how to maximize your technological advances, see **Technology**, p. 119.

EXPANDING YOUR EMPIRE

Each of your bases is constantly building a new unit or base facility. You can decide where a base should direct its industrial efforts. To do so, 🖰 on a base to open the Base Control Screen. In the lower left corner of that screen is a window showing that base's current build orders. 🖰 on the Change button to get the Production Readout, which shows everything your base can build (at the start of the game, this might be just two or three objects). At the start of the game you'll want to concentrate on units. First, build a military unit to guard the base. When it's completed, use ⒣ to order that unit to remain in the base, on guard. If you wish, you may order the base governor to take over production if you 🖰 one of the "Governor" buttons at the top of the Base Control screen (see **Governor**, p. 69).

As soon as the "former" (terraforming) unit becomes available (with the discovery of Centauri Ecology), build one and send it out to terraform the landscape. Move the former out of your base and have it build farms (Ⓕ), roads (Ⓡ), and solar collectors (Ⓢ). If the terrain is harsh (a brown square with no green), plant forests (Shift Ⓕ). If the terrain is rough (lots of grey blobs in the square) drill mines (Ⓜ). You can also automate a former by pressing (Shift Ⓐ); it immediately begins building terrain enhancements as the former commander sees fit.

You'll also want to build some extra colony pods to establish new bases. When a pod is ready, send it out to an inviting green square at least three or four squares away from any other base (and on a river or a coast if possible). [B] builds a new base on that square.

As your faction discovers new technology, you gain an ever wider variety of build options to choose from. Once you have a defensive unit and a former, and have sent out a colony pod from a base, you'll probably want to start improving the base itself by building facilities. Particularly useful facilities for new bases in the early part of the game include the Network Node, Perimeter Defense, Children's Creche, Recycling Tanks and Recreation Commons.

Eventually, when you feel one of your bases is well established, you may want to commit it to building a Secret Project. These massive works take a long time to build but yield lasting benefits to your entire faction.

DIPLOMACY

Inevitably, you come into contact with one of the other factions from the *Unity*. When this happens, you'll usually get a message that the leader of the faction wishes to speak to you, via your commlinks. It's usually a good idea to talk to another leader when given the opportunity. Leaders may offer to trade technologies (often a good idea), or offer you a treaty, or even an alliance (a very good idea, unless you're itching for a fight). On the other hand, they might threaten you or even try to extort energy (the currency of Planet) or technology from you. Giving in to such demands can be humbling, but is sometimes better than the alternative (a fight you may not be ready for). Sometimes they want to borrow energy credits (a good deal in the long run, unless you're going to need the energy you're loaning away in the immediate future).

FACTIONAL STRIFE

Unfortunately, diplomacy can't solve all problems. Sooner or later, you'll have to prepare your faction for armed conflict. Even if your intentions are peaceful, you'll need a standing army, to respond quickly in case of unprovoked aggression. (Keep such defensive forces small—no more than two units per base in the years immediately after Planetfall. Otherwise they'll become expensive to maintain, and rapidly become obsolete.)

If you prefer the conqueror's role, you can put your whole faction on a military footing, building multiple units per base for a massive invasion force. Obviously, you probably shouldn't invest too much time and resources into an operation until you've encountered the enemy and know where they're located.

THE TURN

Sid Meier's Alpha Centauri is a turn-based game. Each turn corresponds to one Chiron year. Mission Year 2100, Planetfall, is the first Chiron year.

Each turn follows the same pattern.

1. **Planet & Enemy Faction move.** All native and enemy units make their moves (including attacks). You see any such movements that fall within the limits of your sensors. The leaders of the other factions may contact you.

2. **Faction Update.** You are advised of any completed enhancements, research or units. (You can customize your preferences for updates; see **Warning Preferences**, p.199.) You may set a new goal for each base when a project is completed, or you may use the defaults. As time progresses, you are offered opportunities to upgrade units, and may receive updates of your progress at unraveling the secrets of this new world.

3. **Player Move.** You (and all other player-controlled factions, in multiplayer games) may move units at this time. You are taken, in turn, to each unit that is:

   • not "holding" in a defensive position, or "asleep" within a transport unit.

   • not already engaged in a multi-turn action.

During this time, you may also freely change your preferences, or change orders to bases or any units (whether or not they're already engaged in orders), contact other faction leaders, inspect visible portions of the map, and review all available data.

GETTING AROUND

The first things you have to learn, in order to establish your faction, are how to interpret the map and how to move around.

The main map, which occupies the top two-thirds of the screen, is your playing surface. At Planetfall (when your faction first arrives on Planet, and when the game begins), the vast bulk of the map is either indistinct or totally black (depending on how you set the *Unity* Survey option; see **Game Rules**, p. 197). You have to move units around and explore to find out exactly what your surroundings are.

The simplest way to move a unit is with the numeric keypad.

The direction in which the keypad arrow points corresponds directly to the direction the unit moves, so that [8] on the numeric keypad moves you one square to the north, while [3] moves you one square to the southeast.

It is also possible to set units to undertake longer, multi-turn journeys without further orders, or even to have them decide for themselves what actions to take. These options are described under the **Action Menu** (p. 92).

Continual movement [Ctrl]+arrow key

If you want a unit to move continually in a single direction, use this command. The unit continues in the specified direction until it can no longer proceed, due to coastlines or enemy units. The unit's commander may route around small obstacles like fungus and small bodies of water.

MOUSE MOVEMENT

If you're sending a unit on a long journey, and you don't want to hit an arrow key for every square of the distance, you can set a destination using the mouse: Just 🖰 (left-click) on the unit, drag to its destination, then release.

The unit figures the most direct path to your destination, automatically routing around obstacles like small bodies of water and fungal areas.

Waypoints. There may be times when you don't want a unit to take the most direct route to its final destination (for example, if a route would take you through hostile territory). In those cases you can use waypoints. To set a waypoint, 🖰-and-drag to the first waypoint square, Spacebar while holding the click, then drag to the next waypoint or to your final destination. A waypoint is set on that square—the unit goes to the waypoint, then on to the next waypoint (if there is another one) or its final destination. A unit will normally follow the path shown on the screen when its orders are given, but it may deviate somewhat based upon the tactical situation at the time it makes the actual move. It always traverses the waypoints in the order given. You can insert up to three waypoints on a route, including the destination.

21

EXAMINING THE MAP

The main map is scrollable. 🖰 (left-click) on any square to center the map on that square. You can also scroll the map in the indicated direction by moving your mouse cursor to the edge of the screen (unless you choose to disable this option).

- If you have a unit in that square, 🖰 also moves your cursor to that square and activates the unit (see **Active Units**, p. 22). If you have multiple units in a square, you choose which unit to activate.

- If you have a base in the square, 🖰 opens the Base Control Screen (see pg. 66).

🖰 (right-click) on a square to open a window containing many of the most commonly used commands. These commands are fully described under **Action Menu**, p. 92.

FOG OF WAR

On any given turn playing with the default game options, there are three types of terrain visible on the map.

Black squares are squares you have not mapped yet. (If you have the *Unity* Survey option turned on, these are not black, but you won't be able to see any details of the square's terrain, other than whether it's land or sea).

Dim squares are those you have already mapped, but which are not currently observed by any of your sensors (either from units or bases).

Bright squares are those you've mapped, and which are currently monitored by your sensors. Most units can observe only adjacent squares. All bases and your units with Deep Radar (a unit special ability) can observe out to two squares away.

ACTIVE UNITS

22

During a turn, each of your units not currently under orders will become active and remain so until you either give it an order or activate a different unit. Active units are shown by a marker or by flashing, depending on the game options you have selected. A unit that has been skipped during your turn because you chose to activate a different unit will re-activate before the end of your turn as a reminder that it still needs instructions. If you are viewing the map, press V to auto-select the next active unit.

COMMLINK

Although it may take awhile to find them, eventually you'll need to communicate with other faction leaders. The commlink system is your means of communication and your tool for trade and diplomacy.

The Commlink button is located on the right edge of your screen.

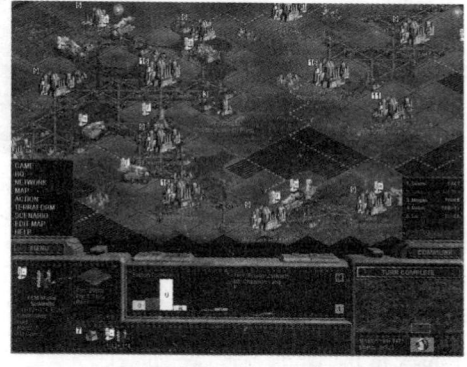

🖰 on this tab or press F12 to open the Commlink menu which displays the names of each of the opposing faction leaders along with your current diplomatic status with that faction (Vendetta, Truce, Treaty, Pact; see **Diplomatic Relations**, p. 129). 🖰 on a name to contact that leader (see **Diplomatic Contact**, p. 127).

A final option, COUNCIL, cannot be used until you have the commlink frequencies for all other leaders. It allows you to convene the Planetary Council. (See **Planetary Council**, p. 132.)

TURN COMPLETE

This button, just below the Commlink tab, allows you to disregard any remaining actions and end the turn (if you have actions left in the turn, you are prompted to confirm your choice). This button flashes when all your units have received orders for the current turn.

WORLD VIEW

The World View map is in the lower right corner of your screen. It displays the world as it is currently known to your faction.

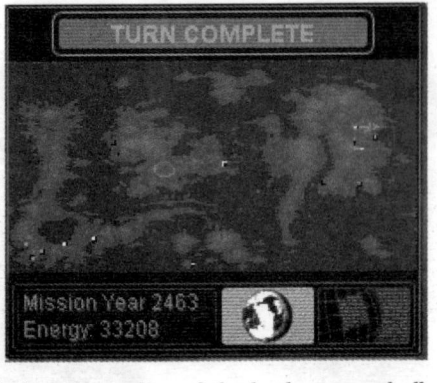

There are two options for viewing your World View map, selected via the buttons beneath the map:

- **World Map** (default view). Displays the outline of the land areas and all known cities by the color of their faction. Double-🖰 an area in the World Map to zoom to the Detail Map (see below).

- **Detail Map.** Displays a close-up of the terrain, so you can keep your eye on potential trouble spots. Double-🖰 an area in the Detail Map to take you back to the World Map (see above).

You can scroll around either view—🖰 on any terrain on the map. The map re-centers where you clicked. 🖰 on the World View in either mode to bring up a menu of options for changing the view.

YEAR/ENERGY

At the bottom of the World View is a readout line showing the current year and your faction's current energy reserves (see **Base Management: The Essentials**, p. 58).

STATUS VIEW

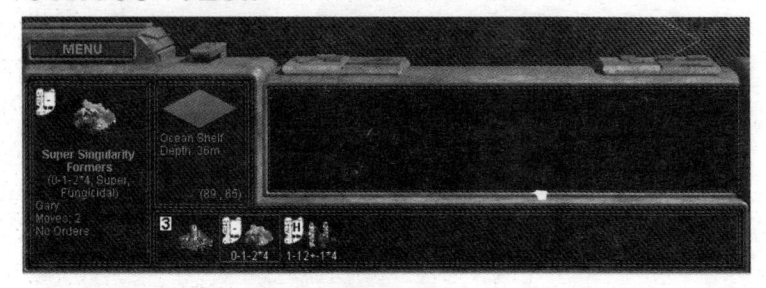

This display comprises the three windows in the lower left corner of the screen. It displays all the essential information about both the active unit and the active square.

The top left window displays information about the active unit or base, if any, including:

- Picture (with status bar)

- Type

- Stats (see **Units**, p. 64)

- Morale Level (see **Morale/Lifecycle**, p. 87)

- Supporting Base

- Move Remaining

- Current Orders (if any) and time to completion (if a terraforming project is underway)

- Base build orders

The top right window displays information about the current square, including:

- Elevation

- Terrain Type (see **Resources,** p. 36)

- Any Enhancements (see **Terraforming and Enhancements,** p. 46)

- Coordinates (see **Mapping Planet,** below)

🖱 on the window to show the number of resources produced by that square.

The long window at the bottom of the screen displays a picture of each unit or base stacked in the current square. Place the cursor over an item to view its data. 🖱 on a picture to make a unit the active unit. 🖱 on a base to zoom to the Base Control Screen.

DATA MFD

This is the window located in the lower center of your screen. It's a repository for general information about your faction and current events.

If you 🖱 on the **M button** (for "messages"), the Data MFD displays the most recent messages generated by the game, with the oldest at the top.

If you 🖱 on the **I button** (for "information"), the Data MFD displays a continuously cycling series of screens displaying important information about your faction and its status among the other factions.

MAPPING PLANET

When you first arrive on Planet, you'll have no idea where you are, where the other factions are, or indeed what might lie over the horizon. You'll have to begin the fascinating process of exploring Planet, and as you progress the world map is unveiled.

The map of Planet is a spherical surface projected onto a rectangular image. This means, in realistic terms, that the squares at the top and bottom of the map (near the poles) represent much smaller areas than the squares in the middle (near the equator). In game terms, however, there's no difference—a square is a square. Understanding the projection, however, does make it easier to understand that the long stretches of rough land at the top and bottom of the screen represent the edge of Planet's uninhabitable polar regions.

MAP COORDINATES

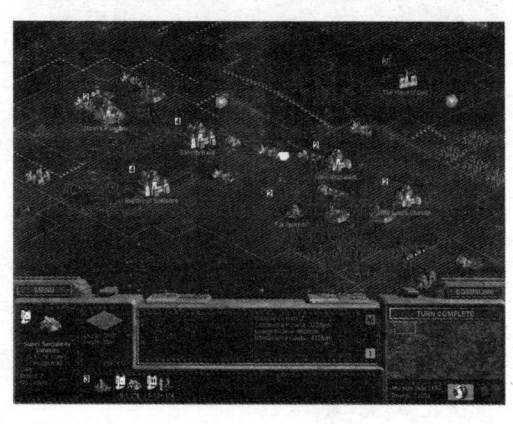

Map coordinates are numbered starting from (0, 0), with the vertical axis first. The vertical axis is numbered from the top of the map to the bottom, and the horizontal is numbered from left to right, starting at the point where the World View (see **World View**, p. 24) wraps. Thus (14, 22) would be nearer the upper left corner of the World View, while (101, 77) would be much lower and farther to the right.

27

ARCHIPELAGOES

Some land squares are connected by a thin line between their diagonal corners, with water squares on either side of this line. These squares are connected by an archipelago of small islands, and these intersections can be crossed both by sea units (from one water square to the other), and by land units (along the archipelago).

MENUS

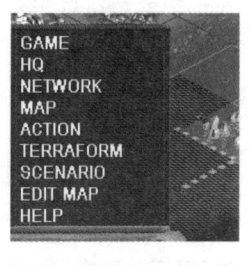

Along the left side of your screen is a tab labeled MENU. 🖰 on the tab, and a list of nine sub-menus appears.

- Game (see **Game Menu**, next page)

- HQ (see **HQ Menu**, p. 110)

- Network (see **Install Guide**)

- Map (see **Map Menu**, p. 32)

- Action (see **Action Menu**, p. 92)

- Terraform (see **Terraform Menu**, p. 46)

- Scenario (see **Scenario and Edit Map Menus**, p. 206)

- Edit Map (see **Scenario and Edit Map Menus**, p. 206)

- Help (see **Help Menu**, p. 31)

From these menus, you can access most of the commands, options and preferences available in the game. Some of the options listed may not appear, either because you have "Simple menus" toggled on (see **Game Menu**, below) or because you cannot carry out a particular order.

GAME MENU

This menu controls the basic functions of the game. There are six preference options, plus a toggle for detailed and simple menu options. The six preference options are:

- Simple\Detailed menu toggle

- Preferences

- Warning Preferences

- Advanced Preferences

- Automation Preferences

- Audio/Visual Preferences

- Map Display Preferences

The various preference menus are discussed in detail in **Appendix** 3, beginning on p. 196. The Simple\Detailed menu toggle controls the level of detail in your Map, Action and Terraform menus. Simple menus show only the basic commands needed to play the game. Detailed menus offer many functions for advanced users.

SAVE GAME

Allows you to create a permanent, named saved game (as opposed to auto-saves—see **Automatic Saves**, p. 30).

When you select this option you are prompted to provide a name for your saved game.

LOAD GAME

Allows you to select a saved game (either named or autosaved) to replace the current game.

RESIGN

A more involved version of the Quit option, Resign totals up your score and shows a replay of the entire game (a graphical display of each faction's advances and losses) before quitting.

START NEW GAME

Quits the current game and returns you to the Start Game menus.

QUIT

Simply closes the game and returns you to the Windows desktop. Progress is saved up through the end of the last complete turn. If you have selected the "Iron Man" option during game setup, your progress will be saved from the moment you quit.

AUTOMATIC SAVES

The game saves itself between each turn. At any given time you can reload the game as it was 1, 2, 3, 4, 5, 10, 20 and 30 turns ago. These saves can all be accessed through the Load Game options at startup or from the Game menu. Automatic saves are stored in the AUTO subdirectory of your SAVES directory.

The "Iron Man" option (see **Game Rules**, p. 197) turns off automatic saves, except when quitting a game, for those who think autosaves make it too easy to go back and undo embarrassing mistakes. If you manually save an Iron Man game, you exit the game.

HELP MENU

This menu opens a comprehensive database of in-depth information about every aspect of the rules, mechanics and background of *Sid Meier's Alpha Centauri*.

The first options in the Help menu open to directories of information about specific aspects of the game, including:

- Index
- General Concepts
- Advanced Concepts
- Technologies
- Base Facilities
- Secret Projects
- Social Engineering

- Factions
- Basic Unit Types
- Chassis Types
- Weapon Types
- Defense Types
- Reactor Types
- Special Abiities

Of special interest to new players are the five "Tours" at the bottom of the menu. These use your current game to walk you through some of the most important aspects of game play, including:

- Interface Tour
- Terraforming Tour
- Base Control Tour
- Social Engineering Tour
- Design Workshop Tour
- Drone Riot Details
- About *Sid Meier's Alpha Centauri* (credits)
- Show Version Number

31

MAP MENU

The Map menu allows you to control how the game displays the main map. Note that if you have the Simple menu option selected (see **Game Menu**, p. 29), you may not get all of these choices.

Move Units (or View Map) [V]

Toggles your main map between View Map Mode and Move Units mode. In Move Units mode you automatically are taken to your current active unit. If you lose track of where you left off your turn while moving around the map, pressing [V] once or twice returns you to your active unit. In View Map mode you can move freely about the map, examining all visible features. You can move your cursor around the map just as you would a unit, using the numerical keypad or the mouse.

Zoom In [Z]

Moves you "closer" to the map's surface, allowing you to view a smaller area at greater detail.

32

Zoom Out [X]

Moves you "further" from the map's surface, allowing you to view a larger area at less detail.

Standard Zoom In [Shift][Z]

Takes you to a median zoom level that should be comfortable for playing.

Standard Zoom Out [Shift][X]

Takes you to a median zoom level somewhat "further out" than Standard Zoom In, but still comfortable for playing.

Full Zoom In [Ctrl][Z]

Zooms you in as far as possible.

Full Zoom Out [Ctrl][X]

Zooms you out as far as possible.

Toggle Flattened Terrain [Ctrl] [Shift] [X]

Toggles the map's topographic perspective on or off, allowing you to see mountain and valley squares from either 2- or 3-D perspective.

Toggle Map Grid [Ctrl] [G]

Toggles the map grid (faint gray lines separating individual squares).

Toggle Base Grid [Ctrl] [Shift] [G]

Toggles a red border that marks the "production radius" of bases in the game (see **Working the Land**, p. 60).

Show Autoforward Routes [Ctrl] [Shift] [B]

Autoforward routes automatically move units from one base to another (see **Action Menu**, p. 46). This toggle shows the routes you have implemented.

Show Patrol Orders [Shift] [P]

Toggles a dotted green line along the routes of your patrolling units (see **Action Menu**, p. 46).

33

Terrain Survey [T]

Changes all the bases, units, and terrain features on the map between invisible and visible, allowing you to view the terrain without obstruction. Selecting this option consecutive times removes additional terrain features.

Hide/Show Names & Production [Ctrl] [N]

Cycles the name and current production orders displayed beneath each base. This command cycles between no names, names only, and names and production orders.

Name Landmark [Shift] [N]

Allows you to assign a name to a given region. Select the square to be named and select this option. You are prompted to enter a name. The name is applied to the target square and its adjacent squares.

Erase Landmark [Ctrl][Shift][N]

Deletes the name of a previously named region. Place the cursor in any square within the named region and 🖰 this option. You are prompted to confirm your choice.

Locate Base [Ctrl][B]

Presents you with a list of all your current bases. 🖰 on one to display its position on the World Map (see **World View**, p. 24). This list also contains several option buttons.

- **Sort: Name** Sorts your bases alphabetically by name (this is the default).

- **Sort: Size** Sorts your bases from largest to smallest.

- **Sort: Dist** Sorts your bases from nearest to farthest from the current active square.

- **Zoom** Opens the Base Control Screen (see p. 66) for the selected base.

- **OK** Saves the current sort preference as the default and closes the screen.

- **Cancel** Closes the screen.

Previous Cursor Position [Bksp]

Cycles you backwards through your recent cursor positions.

Next Cursor Position [Shift][Bksp]

Cycles you forwards through your recent cursor positions (only functional if you have already cycled back one or more steps).

Center Screen [C]

Centers the screen on your cursor position.

CHAPTER 3

PLANET

PLANET

Before you can turn your attention to the old terrestrial games of politics and warfare, you must first focus on the serious business of surviving and thriving on a strange world. Unlike the human factions, Planet cannot be conquered, dominated or negotiated with, but it can be worked with to ensure the survival and prosperity of your people.

RESOURCES

Resources are the essential elements which you extract from your surroundings to support and expand your faction. There are three types of resource—nutrients, which support your population and allow your bases to grow in size; minerals, which allow you to build units and facilities; and energy, the currency of Planet.

To obtain the resources from any given square, it must be inside your territory (see **Working the Land**, p. 60), inside the production radius of a base (within a two-square radius, excluding diagonals), and that base must assign a unit of its population to work that square (see **Working the Land**, p. 60). Unworked squares yield no resources, regardless of their fertility.

Your ability to exploit territory is limited by your technology. When you first arrive on Planet, you are generally unable to recover more than two of any one resource per turn (see **Resource Production Tables**, p. 52). As you acquire new technologies, your production capacity expands until you are fully able to exploit the resource potential of every square in a base's production radius.

NUTRIENTS (RAINFALL)

For your faction to increase, you must be able to extract healthy nutrients from the alien ecosystem of Planet. The more nutrients a base produces, the faster and larger it can grow. Rainfall directly determines the amount of nutrients a square can produce.

There are three levels of rainfall on Planet—**arid**, **moist** and **rainy**. Rainy squares show as green on the map, and are usually the best places to establish new bases. Arid squares show up as brown, and moist squares combine green and brown. When scouting for new settlements, always remember, "Green is good."

Without any modifiers (such as special resources, enhancements, xenofungus, monoliths and others, all detailed below), an arid square produces no nutrients, a moist square produces 1 nutrient per turn, and a rainy square produces 2 nutrients. Rocky squares (see **Minerals**, p. 37) do not produce nutrients regardless of rainfall.

Moist and rainy squares are excellent places to build farms to enhance nutrient production. The amount of nutrients any given square can produce is limited until the discovery of Gene Splicing.

MINERALS (ROCKINESS)

Mineral production controls the rate at which your bases improve, as well as your ability to produce military, transport and terraforming units. Existing units may also require a certain amount of mineral raw materials for support.

The rockier a square, the more minerals it produces. There are three levels of rockiness—**flat**, **rolling** and **rocky**. Without any modifiers (such as special resources, enhancements, xenofungus, monoliths and others, all detailed below), a flat square produces no minerals, while a rolling or rocky square produces 1 mineral per turn.

Bases cannot be established in rocky squares, nor can farms be started there. They are, however, excellent places for mines. For more details, see **Terraform Menu**, p. 46.

The amount of minerals any given square can produce is limited until the discovery of Ecological Engineering.

ENERGY (ELEVATION)

A solar collector must be built in a square to harvest its energy from elevation. Energy allows you to sustain your bases in working order. Even more importantly, though, it is the effective currency of the human factions of Planet.

The energy you collect is allocated to three different areas: Economy, Labs and Psych. Energy allocated to Economy is used to maintain base facilities; any excess is placed in the energy reserve. Your faction's economic power is measured by its energy reserves. These reserves are saved in the form of "energy credits," and are used for maintaining base facilities, commerce and energy payments between factions. Energy from the energy reserves may also be invested in mineral production to hurry projects to completion (see **Build Orders**, p. 67). Energy allocated to Labs speeds research into new technologies (see **Energy Allocation**, p. 117). Energy allocated to Psych helps maintain order in your bases (see **Energy Allocation**, p. 117).

Squares with solar collectors produce 1 energy per level of elevation. There are four levels of elevation above sea level on the Planet–0 to **1,000 meters** above sea level, **1,000 to 2,000 meters**, **2,000 to 3,000 meters**, and **above 3,000 meters**. For example, a solar collector built in a square at 1025 m would produce 2 energy each turn. You can find the elevation of a square by checking it in the **Status View** (p. 25). You can also see elevations and depressions on the map.

The amount of energy any given square can produce is limited until the discovery of Environmental Economics.

CLIMATE AND ELEVATION

The rainfall of a given region is partly determined by the elevation of the surrounding terrain. On Planet, the prevailing winds always blow from west to east. This means that the westward exposure of a ridge or mountainside catches more airborne moisture–the effective rainfall increases on that side. However, little moisture reaches the eastward slope, so the rainfall decreases on that side. A great mountain range may be lush and green on the western side, but will be arid desert on the eastern side.

You can learn to exploit this pattern by raising and lowering terrain with your former units to create favorable rainfall conditions for yourself or unfavorable rainfall for an opponent (see **Terraform Menu**, p. 46).

NATIVE LIFE

Planet has been teeming with life since eons before the arrival of humanity. Individual specimens of Planet's indigenous species seem simpler than analogous Earth life, but appearances can be deceiving. Much of Planet's plant and animal life is tied together in a grand symbiotic relationship, far more intricate than any comparable system on Earth. Truly the whole is greater than the sum of its parts. For more information on the native ecology of Planet, see **Planetography**, p. 216.

FLORA

Though there are many different species of plant life, the dominant form is the crimson, fantastically shaped **xenofungus** (or "fungus"), which covers vast tracts of the surface. Its near cousin, **sea fungus**, is equally ubiquitous in Planet's oceans and seas.

Fungus squares (squares with fungus in them) can not be used for bases, tend to spawn mind worm boils (see **Fauna**, p. 40), and they are difficult to move through. However they do have one useful property—a ground or sea unit can hide in a fungus or sea fungus square, and is invisible to detection by all other factions unless they actually try to move a unit into the square or have sensor arrays nearby (see **Terraform Menu**, p. 46). Also, units attacked while in fungus get a defensive bonus, unless the attacking unit is itself native life (either human-bred or "wild;" see **Fauna**, p. 40), in which case the attacking unit gets an offensive bonus.

As your knowledge of Planet expands, you discover ways to extract useful resources from fungus squares (see **Resource Production Table**, p. 52). You can also overcome many of the inconveniences of fungus squares by enhancing your Planet rating through Social Engineering (see **Social Factors**, p. 141), allowing easier movement through fungus.

Bases and enhancements cannot be built on xenofungus squares, but the resources of the fungus itself can be harvested. As your terraforming technology improves, you acquire the ability to clear, and even to cultivate xenofungus. Fungus can be planted to create defensive barriers, or simply for the resources it yields.

FAUNA

The dominant animal life of Planet is the **mind worm**, a horrid-looking little parasitic carnivore about 10 cm long. A single mind worm is a dangerous pest, able to burrow into a human brain and devour it, while the victim succumbs to violent delusions or dangerous fantasies, or lives out his deepest terrors. Many theories have been advanced to explain the psychoactive nature of these attacks but none have been experimentally validated.

Far worse than a single worm, mind worms are known to form vast mobile colonies, called "boils," which can overwhelm a military unit or a whole human base.

In addition to the land-based boils, there is also an aquatic vector for mind worms called the **Isle of the Deep**. This floating terror can attack ships at sea. It can also attack coastlines, spitting up mind worm boils on shore. Even an airborne vector, poetically dubbed the **Locusts of Chiron**, haunts Planet's stratosphere.

All three mind worm vectors go through a lifecycle. Seven different phases of growth for each vector have been identified (See **Morale/Lifecycle**, p. 87). The larger and more mature a boil, the more dangerous it is.

As your technology advances and your knowledge of Planet increases, you might acquire the ability to grow native life-forms and place them under your control for use as weapons. You may also acquire the ability to enslave wild mind worm boils into your service.

TERRAIN

The fantastic vistas of Planet offer more than alien beauty. Planet provides an endless variety of both gifts and pitfalls for the human settlers.

RIVERS

Since the dawn of human history, rivers have been the arteries of civilization. This remains true on Planet. If a river runs through a square, it delivers a +1 bonus to energy production. Rivers also tend to increase the moisture of the squares they run through or by. Rivers start from an underground source and follow the contours of the land down to the sea. With the proper technology you can tap into underground aquifers and create new rivers.

Rivers can also be used as natural roads. A unit can float up or down three river squares for every one square of normal movement it possesses.

OCEANS

There are three types of ocean terrain (corresponding to the three elevations of land terrain): **ocean shelf**, **ocean**, and **ocean trench**. With the proper technologies and equipment, ocean shelf squares can be improved, and aquatic bases can be established there. Ocean and ocean trench squares can not support bases or be enhanced.

41

RESOURCE SPECIALS

 The ecology of Planet is complex, and a few regions produce significantly more nutrients, energy or minerals than would be expected from their moisture, elevation or rockiness. These special squares are indicated by icons, indicating the type of resource that is increased in that square.

UNITY PODS AND MONOLITHS

Before the *Unity* was destroyed, it released the Colony Pods of the seven factions and scores of robotic "seed pods," carrying vital supplies and technology for humanity's conquest of the new world. Unfortunately, because of the chaos in the last hours of the *Unity*, these pods were scattered at random over Planet's surface.

Many of the *Unity* pods became infested with indigenous life-forms and opening them unleashes fungal blooms or mind worm boils. A few others react unpredictably with Planet itself, triggering massive earthquakes. The majority, however, continue to hold valuable resources such as units and information from old Earth.

Far more mysterious are the monoliths, relics of a mysterious intelligence that visited or inhabited Planet long before humanity's invasion. The monoliths possess amazing psycho-technical powers. They can completely repair units that are damaged and even make improvements to those units' performance. However, a monolith can enhance only so many units before its mysterious power is exhausted and it ceases to exist.

Monolith squares yield two of each sort of resource, regardless of the underlying terrain (until the monolith disappears).

Other relics of the past are the alien artifacts—mobile machines that seem to be a form of computer. Artifacts can be linked to Network Nodes to discover new technologies, or their power can be tapped to hasten the completion of Secret Projects.

Most of the time, monoliths and alien artifacts are indistinguishable from *Unity* pods to long-range sensors. Only by actually sending a unit into the square to open the pod can it be determined if the pod is a useful gift from the *Unity*, an alien relic, or a disaster waiting to happen.

FORESTS

One of the fundamental advantages of formers is their ability to plant forests of terrestrial vegetation on the more inhospitable regions of Planet. Forests provide a small yield of nutrients and minerals, while doing no damage to the ecology of Planet (in fact, forest can actually offset ecological damage from enhanced squares). Over time, forest squares expand into adjacent undeveloped squares. When a forest is harvested—that is, when any enhancement other than a road is built on it—you receive a one-time bonus of +5 minerals.

Planting forests is an excellent method of deriving benefit from arid terrain, particularly early in the game before some of the more advanced terraforming options are available.

FUNGUS

The ubiquitous xenofungus can produce resources when you discover the appropriate technology:

- **Centauri Ecology** gives you one nutrient per fungus square (per turn).

- **Centauri Meditation** gives you one energy per fungus square (per turn).

- **Centauri Genetics** gives you one mineral per fungus square (per turn).

- **Centauri Psi** gives you one more nutrient per fungus square (per turn).

- **Secrets of Alpha Centauri** gives you one more energy per fungus square (per turn).

- Terraformers can plant xenofungus after the discovery of **Ecological Engineering**; sea terraformers can plant sea fungus with this discovery.

LANDMARKS

Landmarks are giant natural wonders of Planet, the most important geophysical features of the world. You *might* encounter any of the following.

Freshwater Sea. The richest aquatic region on Planet provides +1 nutrient per square.

Garland Crater. Some thousands of years ago, a massive object crashed into Planet, leaving this vast crater. The rare and valuable remnants of the original object remain in the crater, giving the squares inside a +1 mineral bonus.

Geothermal Shallows. A whole field of underwater geysers underlies this coastal shelf, providing +1 energy per square.

Great Dunes. The largest, most unforgiving desert on Planet. The Great Dunes provide no bonus resources, and are in fact a remarkably inhospitable place.

Monsoon Jungle. This is an anomalous expanse of thick and curiously earthlike vegetation. The rich soil of the Monsoon Jungle yields +1 nutrient per square.

Mount Planet. This enormous volcano is active, but its slopes provide a +1 bonus of both minerals and energy. The enormous crater at the top fills a whole square with lava.

New Sargasso. This is the largest naturally occurring growth of sea fungus on Planet. It provides no special bonus, other than the resources that can be harvested from the fungus itself.

Pholus Ridge. The geothermal energy unleashed by the clash of two of Planet's tectonic plates produces +1 energy per square along Pholus Ridge.

Sunny Mesa. This extensive highland offers no special resource bonuses, but its elevation makes it naturally excellent for harvesting energy.

The Ruins. A vast and ancient ring of monoliths embedded in thick xenofungus, it has no special resources, other than the monoliths themselves.

Uranium Flats. This savanna is particularly rich in heavy elements that provide +1 energy per square.

HOW TERRAIN AFFECTS MOVEMENT

A unit's current movement points are displayed in the status view. As the unit moves, this number decreases as movement points are used up.

Certain terrain types impede normal movement (these penalties have no effect if moving across the square on a road or mag tube).

Rocky and forest squares each cost two movement points to cross, while sea fungus squares drain three movement points (however, these squares can always be entered by any unit having at least one full movement point remaining).

Trying to enter a land fungus square (successfully or not) always ends your unit's movement, unless the unit is a mind worm boil, or your faction possesses the Xenoempathy Dome Secret Project.

Rivers are important in planning movement over undeveloped terrain, because of their ability to triple a unit's normal move.

Terrain has no effect on the movement of air units.

45

HOW TERRAIN AFFECTS COMBAT

Terrain can, in specific situations, provide crucial advantages in combat to savvy commanders and deadly pitfalls to the unwary.

The important tactical ability of xenofungus to provide concealment has already been discussed (**Flora**, p. 39).

Artillery units (see **Artillery Combat**, p. 100) get an offensive bonus of +25% per level of altitude from which they are attacking.

Mobile units in smooth or rolling terrain get a +25% offensive bonus, reflecting their ability to make the most of their agility.

Any unit in rocky terrain gets a +50% defensive bonus.

Any unit in xenofungus gets a +50% defensive bonus, unless it is being attacked by a native life-form (either human-spawned or "wild") in which case the unit gets no defensive bonus, but the native life-form gets a +50% combat bonus.

TERRAFORMING AND ENHANCEMENTS

Terraforming literally means "to make earthlike." It is the art of maximizing resource production in a given area, making that square more hospitable to human life. It involves building technological enhancements to the square or, in extreme cases, actually changing the terrain itself. Terraforming operations must be carried out by former units, which become available upon discovery of Centauri Ecology.

TERRAFORM MENU

Terraforming actions are listed on the Terraform menu. Some actions on the menu require the discovery of certain technologies before the action becomes available; you see only the options allowed by your current technology on the menu. If an action is possible, the menu indicates the estimated time in turns required to complete it. The construction rates listed below are normal values and decrease as your terraforming technology and equipment improves. Note that the longer an enhancement takes to build, the more ecological damage it causes (see **Ecological Risks**, p. 54). Also, if you have the Simple menu option selected (see **Game Menu**, p. 29), you may not get all of these choices.

SQUARE ENHANCEMENT LIMITATIONS

Terraformers may construct facilities in individual squares to *enhance* the resource output of that square or to enhance the performance of the square in other ways. In general, a square may contain a road or mag-tube, a farm/soil enricher, and one additional enhancement. Building an enhancement in a square that contains any enhancement other than a farm (or soil enricher) and road (or mag tube) destroys the earlier enhancement.

CULTIVATE FARM/KELP FARM [F]   RATE 4

A farm increases nutrient production by one; kelp farms (that is, farms in the ocean) increase nutrient production by two. Farms can be built only on land squares that are not rocky, occupied by xenofungus, or contain a monolith. A kelp farm may be built only on ocean shelf squares.

Building a farm requires Centauri Ecology. Building a kelp farm also requires Doctrine: Flexibility.

CONSTRUCT SOIL ENRICHER [F]   RATE 8

Enrichers may be built only on land squares containing farms. They increase the nutrient production of the farm by one.

Requires Advanced Ecological Engineering.

CONSTRUCT MINE/MINING PLATFORM [M]   RATE 8

Mining increases mineral production by +1 in flat or rolling squares and +2 in rocky squares, but they reduce nutrient output by one if the square would ordinarily produce more than one. A road in a mined rocky square adds an additional +1 to the square's mineral output. Mining platforms increase mineral production by +1 in ocean squares until the discovery of Advanced Ecological Engineering; they add +2 minerals thereafter. Mines cannot be built in squares occupied by xenofungus or a monolith. Mining platforms may be built only on ocean shelf squares.

Building a mine requires Centauri Ecology. Building a mining platform also requires Doctrine: Flexibility.

CONSTRUCT SOLAR COLLECTOR/TIDAL HARNESS [S]
RATE 6 (+2 IN ROCKY)/4 (TIDAL HARNESS)

A solar collector (or a tidal harness on an ocean shelf) increases energy production. Solar collectors produce one energy per level of altitude (see Energy/Elevation, p. 38), while tidal harnesses produce +2 energy on ocean shelf squares. Solar collectors cannot be built in squares containing xenofungus or a monolith.

Building a solar collector requires Centauri Ecology. Building a tidal harness also requires Doctrine: Flexibility.

PLANT FOREST [Shift][F]
RATE 4

A forest of terran trees provides a limited but steady supply of nutrients and minerals, regardless of the underlying terrain. Forests spread to adjacent undeveloped squares over time. Forest can not be planted in squares containing enhancements other than a road or mag tube. Tree Farm and Hybrid Forest facilities increase the resources available from forest squares inside the base's production radius.

BUILD ROAD [R]
RATE 1 (+1 FOR RIVER, +2 FUNGUS, +2 FOREST, +1 ROCKY, CUMULATIVE)

Roads speed movement at a rate of three road squares for every one square of normal movement. Roads can be built only in land squares devoid of xenofungus until the discovery of Centauri Empathy, which allows roads to traverse xenofungus.

BUILD MAG TUBE [R]
RATE DEPENDS ON TERRAIN

Mag tubes are the heavy transit system of the future, utilizing magnetic forces to push passenger and cargo modules through a vacuum tube at near hypersonic speeds. Movement by mag tube is free, allowing a unit to move from any square with a mag tube to any other square connecting to that mag tube, as long as that unit has movement points remaining. Mag tubes may be built in any square containing a road.

Requires Monopole Magnets.

CONSTRUCT BUNKER [K]
RATE 5

Bunkers are defensive fortifications that can be built on any land square. They increase the defensive strength of all units inside them and limit the effects of collateral damage (see **Damage**, p. 103).

Requires Advanced Military Algorithms.

CONSTRUCT AIRBASE [Shift][.]
RATE 10

An airbase is a ground facility outside a base where air units can land safely, refuel, repair, and take off again.

Requires Doctrine: Air Power.

CONSTRUCT SENSOR ARRAYS [O]   RATE 4

Sensor arrays allow you to see everything within a two-square radius (including units hiding in fungus). Additionally, a sensor array grants a defensive bonus to your units within its two-square radius. The ownership of a sensor array is determined by the borders of your faction. If your borders move, placing the array outside your boundaries, it may come under control of a new faction.

REMOVE FUNGUS [F]   RATE 6

Exterminates all the xenofungus in the square.

PLANT FUNGUS [Ctrl][F]   RATE 6

Creates a fungus square and destroys enhancements other than roads or mag tubes.

Requires Ecological Engineering.

49

CONSTRUCT CONDENSER [N]   RATE 12

Condensers collect atmospheric moisture for use in irrigation. A condenser acts as a farm, but also increases the moisture level of every square within a two-square radius by +1 (if the square already has a farm or soil enricher, the condenser replaces the farm or enricher.)

Requires Ecological Engineering.

CONSTRUCT ECHELON MIRROR [Shift][E]   RATE 12

An echelon mirror links a series of mirrors into a network. Every square adjacent to the echelon mirror with a solar collector enhancement gets a +1 energy bonus. An echelon mirror may be built on any land square.

Requires Ecological Engineering.

CONSTRUCT THERMAL BOREHOLE [Shift][B]   RATE 24

A thermal borehole is a shaft driven through the crust of Planet to tap directly into the geothermal energy and rare mineral resources of the inner core. A thermal borehole yields +6 minerals and +6 energy, regardless of terrain type. No other enhancements except roads and mag tubes may be built in the same square as a thermal borehole, and they can only be built on land.

Requires Ecological Engineering.

DRILL TO AQUIFER [Q]   RATE 18

This command taps into a subterranean fresh-water source and brings it to the surface. The new water source immediately begins to flow to the sea, creating a river.

Requires Ecological Engineering.

TERRAFORM UP [ ]]   RATE 12

50

You can raise the elevation of a square, raising surrounding squares proportionately, to create a natural slope. Terraforming up can increase energy production in the region and also provide a natural barrier to trap atmospheric moisture (see **Energy/Elevation**, p. 38), increasing rainfall on the windward slope and decreasing it on the downwind side. It can also be used to build land bridges by raising the sea floor.

Requires Environmental Economics.

TERRAFORM DOWN [[ ]   RATE 12

You can lower the elevation of a square, dropping surrounding squares proportionately. Sea formers can lower coastal squares below sea level, turning them into ocean shelf squares (this is done by lowering an ocean shelf square to make it an ocean square—the slope created causes adjacent coastal squares to drop below sea level). This destroys any enhancements and units in the submerged area, as well as any bases not protected by a Pressure Dome facility. This option can be used to destroy land bridges.

Requires Environmental Economics.

TERRAFORM LEVEL [Shift][_]   RATE 8

You can reduce the rockiness in a square by one level per use.

FARM + SOLAR + ROAD [Ctrl][Shift][S]

This command tells the former to build these three enhancements in the square, in sequence, each at their normal rate. If used in a xenofungus square, this command also clears the fungus. If terrain or previous enhancements prevent the completion of all three commands, as many as possible are executed.

FARM + MINE + ROAD [Control][Shift][M]

This command tells the former to build these three enhancements in the square, in sequence, each at their normal rate. If used in a xenofungus square, this command also clears the fungus. If terrain prevents the former from carrying out all three commands, it executes as many as possible.

CONSTRUCT ROAD TO [Ctrl][R]   RATE (DEPENDS ON TERRAIN)

51

The former builds a road directly from its current position to one of your bases. You get a list of bases from which to select the destination for the road.

CONSTRUCT TUBE TO [Ctrl][T]   RATE 3/SQUARE

The former builds a mag tube directly from its current position to one of your bases. You get a list of bases from which to select a destination. Your destination and current position need not already be connected by road—the former builds a road, as well.

AUTOMATIC ROADS [Ctrl][Shift][R]   RATE (DEPENDS ON TERRAIN)

The former builds roads at its commander's discretion.

AUTOMATIC TUBES [Ctrl][Shift][T]   RATE 3/SQUARE

The former builds mag tubes at its own discretion. (It will build both roads and mag tubes in squares that do not already have roads.)

AUTOMATIC SENSORS [Ctrl][Shift][O]   RATE 4/SENSOR

The former builds sensors at its own discretion.

AUTOMATIC FUNGUS REMOVAL [Ctrl][Shift][F]   RATE 6/SQUARE

The former selects squares from which to remove fungus.

AUTOIMPROVE HOME BASE [Ctrl][Shift][A]   RATE VARIABLE

The former automatically makes enhancements within the territory of the unit's home base. If the former is away from its home base, this command starts it moving towards home.

FULLY AUTOMATE FORMER [Shift][A]   RATE
                                        AS INDIVIDUAL ENHANCEMENTS

The former becomes fully self-directed, moving about and taking action as its commander sees fit. (Basic parameters for automated formers can be set using the Preference menus; see **Automation Preferences**, p. 201).

RESOURCE PRODUCTION TABLES

Underlying Terrain	Nutrients	Minerals	Energy
Raininess			
Arid	0		
Moist	1		
Rainy	2		
Rockiness			
Flat		0	
Rolling		1	
Rocky	0[1]	1	
Elevation			1–4[2]
Ocean	1	0	0

Fixed Squares

The production of the following squares is fixed, regardless of underlying terrain.

Underlying Terrain	Nutrients	Minerals	Energy
Base	2	1	2

Note: bases get resource bonuses as well

Forest [3]	1	2	0
Monolith	2	2	2
Thermal Borehole	0	6	6
Fungus [4]	0-2	0-2	0-2

Modifiers

River			+1
Farm	+1		
Kelp Farm	+2		
Soil Enricher	+1		
Condenser	+1 [5]		
Echelon Mirror			+1 [6]
Tidal Harness			+2
Mine	-1 [7]	+1 or 2 [8]	
Road		+1 [9]	
Mining Platform		+1 or 2 [10]	
Nutrient Bonus	+2		
Mineral Bonus		+2	
Energy Bonus			+2
Recycling Tanks [11]	+1	+1	+1

53

[1] Rocky terrain negates all nutrient production from raininess.

[2] In order to harvest energy based on a square's elevation, the square must have a solar collector. Squares with solar collectors yield 1 energy for each thousand meters above sea level, starting at 1 for squares 0 to 1,000 meters above sea level, up to 4 for squares over 3,000 meters above sea level.

[3] Harvesting a forest square (i.e., building any enhancement other than a road in that square) yields a one-time bonus of 5 minerals. Tree Farm and Hybrid Forest facilities each increase nutrient production in forest squares within that base's production radius.

[4] Your ability to extract resources from fungus improves as you acquire new technologies. See **Fungus**, p. 43.

[5] Also raises the raininess by one increment in a two-square radius.

[6] Also provides +1 energy to every adjacent square with a solar collector.

[7] A mine will not reduce nutrient production to zero.

[8] +1 in flat or rolling terrain, +2 in rocky terrain.

[9] Roads provide +1 minerals in rocky squares with a mine (total bonus from road and mine: +3). Roads do not provide a bonus to mines in flat or rolling terrain.

[10] Bonus is +1 until the discovery of Advanced Ecological Engineering, +2 thereafter.

[11] Recycling tanks only affect the central base square.

ECOLOGICAL RISKS

If Planet's complex ecology is not respected, it turns on an invader. Each technological enhancement constructed on any square in a base's production radius increases that base's ecological disruption. In general, the more complex an enhancement (i.e., the longer it takes to complete), the greater the damage it causes. Also, the higher a base's mineral production, the greater the chance of ecological disaster.

Your ecological damage ranking, as shown on your base screen (see **Data Readout**, p. 73), gives the percentage chance on each turn that Planet will react to your disruptions, in the form of uncontrolled fungus blooms that wipe out all existing enhancements in a given square. The new fungal squares also often spawn voracious native life-forms.

Ecological damage can be minimized (or even eliminated entirely) through Social Engineering (increase your Planet rating; see **Social Factors**, p. 141), base facilities (Centauri Preserve, Temple of Planet; see **Facilities**, p. 64) and Secret Projects (The Pholus Mutagen and others; see **Secret Projects**, p. 65).

RANDOM NATURAL PHENOMENA

Planet is a mysterious and complex system. It constantly produces new and unexpected means to discomfit and endanger humanity, but it can also capriciously produce surprising blessings.

The influence of Planet's suns and moons may provoke a burst of mind worm activity, or solar flares may increase energy stores while disrupting diplomatic communications, or you may discover an unexpected store of extra resources near a base, or an alien plague may break out. The effects of random events range from windfalls to disasters. Some events directly affect your faction, others affect other factions, and many affect all of Planet indiscriminately.

Some events happen instantaneously; others last for several years. Negative random events can sometimes be avoided (for example, plagues are far less likely to break out in bases with biology lab facilities), but most just have to be ridden out, for better or worse.

The only thing that can be reliably said about natural phenomenon on Planet is it's always safest to expect the unexpected.

Random events can by turned off in the game configuration options.

CHAPTER 4

COLONIZING PLANET

COLONIZING PLANET

Your faction begins as a few huddled refugees in a single, makeshift encampment. It's up to you to see that it grows into a self-sufficient, globally dominant society.

BASES

Your fundamental goal on Planet is for your faction to survive and thrive. Your faction expands, in terms of size, power and influence, by building new bases. These bases are each independent, self-contained 'cities'—the centers of your faction's economic, military, technological and social progress. A base's production radius extends up to 20 squares surrounding it, up to two squares away excluding diagonals. It is from these squares that the resources are gathered for your faction's consumption.

BASE MANAGEMENT: THE ESSENTIALS

Your bases produce several different types of items, all of which are used in various ways to build your new society. To enter one of your bases, 🖰 on it in the World View.

Base Governor is an intelligent manager that can control your base production for you. The governor can be set to one of four priorities—Explore, Discover, Build or Conquer (see **Governor**, p. 69).

Citizens—the laborers and followers of your faction—populate your bases. These citizens work the surrounding terrain to collect *resources*: nutrients, minerals and energy.

Nutrients feed your people to keep them alive and functioning. Nutrients that are not used directly for this purpose help to grow the base population. Population growth is essential for a strong empire, since more people mean more workers to collect resources.

Minerals represent all raw materials derived from Planet that are used for construction. They are used to build *units* (vehicles and equipment) and base *facilities* (special buildings). They are also used to maintain units (provide spare parts and so on) supported by the base.

- Units are mobile, and may be used for defense, exploration and conquest.

- Facilities increase the capabilities of the base that builds them. Certain one-of-a-kind facilities (see **Secret Projects**, p. 165) can be built only once but benefit your whole faction. Most facilities have a prerequisite technology that you must discover before you can build the facility (see **Facilities**, p. 64).

Energy is collected from the area surrounding your base, from rivers, or by using solar collectors to harness heat (see **Terraform Menu**, p. 46). The energy you collect is allocated for use in three different areas of your bases: *Economy*, *Labs* and *Psych*. (Note that Specialist citizens can increase energy allotments in specific areas; see **Citizens**, p. 61.)

- Energy allocated to Economy is used to maintain base facilities; any excess is placed in the energy reserves. Your faction's economic power is measured by the size of its energy reserves. These reserves are saved as "energy credits," and can be used like money for base facility maintenance, commerce between factions, or to expedite construction projects.

- Energy allocated to Labs speeds research into new technologies.

- Energy allocated to Psych helps maintain order and peaceful existence inside your bases.

- See **Energy Allocation**, p. 117, for more details.

GETTING BASES

When you arrive on Planet, your first base is usually placed for you, depending on your game setup options. Once your first base is established, you can build colony pods to construct others, or acquire bases from other factions through conquest (see **Bases and Facilities**, p. 104), Probe Team activity (see **Mind**

Control, p. 135), or diplomacy (see **Diplomatic Contact, p. 127**). There are two types of bases: those established on land and those established in the sea.

- To build a land base, press ⬚B while a land colony pod is active. This establishes a new base on the square the pod currently occupies. Land bases cannot be established on rocky, fungus or monolith squares.

- Sea colonies can only be established by sea colony pods on ocean squares without sea fungus.

Colony pods can also be used to increase a base's population instantaneously—place a pod in an existing base, and press ⬚B to increase that base's population by one.

Location, Location, Location

Your bases should be placed near good resources, with ample nutrients, minerals and energy available nearby. When founding new bases, remember that green is good — the more green in an area (representing rainfall), the more nutrients may be produced. Green areas of the map almost always make excellent base locations, particularly those that are near rivers, which generate additional energy and expedite the movement of units around the base.

Placing your bases in useful relationship to each other is a very important component of success in *Sid Meier's Alpha Centauri*. Put your bases too close together and they'll cannibalize each other's resources, limiting their growth and economic power. If you spread them out too much, you'll be wasting much of Planet's resources, as well as compromising your ability to defend your territory.

WORKING THE LAND

Each of your bases is a self-contained "city," with an area under its influence up to 20 squares surrounding it, up to two squares away. This is called its "production radius" (see diagram).

Before your base can exploit the resources of any square in its radius, a citizen must be assigned to work it. If a base has a population of five, it can exploit up to five squares in its production radius, in addition to the square

The base's production radius is defined by the area bordered by the red line

it's in (that square is automatically fully utilized, with no need of actually assigning anyone to work it).

You can place your workers by hand (see **Assigning Citizens to Work**, p. 71), or the base governor assigns citizens as he sees fit (see **Governor**, p. 69).

CITIZENS

The human citizens of your bases represent a resource even more vital than energy, minerals or nutrients. While the base governor can handle much of the day-to-day work of citizen allocation, ultimately it is up to you to assign your citizens for the greater good of the faction. Note that each "citizen" represents a thousand or more humans. There are four classes of citizens on Planet: *Workers*, *Talents*, *Drones* and *Specialists*.

Workers are the salt-of-the-Planet, skilled workforce that keeps things running along smoothly.

Talents are the cream that rises to the top of your society, your pool of highly skilled professionals. Talents are created by facilities, Secret Projects, certain specialists, and energy allocated to Psych (each two energy units allocated results in one additional worker becoming a talent; see **Energy Allocation**, p. 117).

Drones are the unskilled, unsuitable and disgruntled among your people. They're lazy troublemakers, and they all carry weapons. Drones have a profound effect upon social order inside a base. See **Drone Riots**, p. 63.

- **Specialists** do not work the outlying squares of the base to harness resources. Instead, they work inside the base, adding directly to the base's Economy, Psych and Labs production (see **Energy Allocation**, p. 117).

Until the base has sufficient population to work every single square in its production radius, you have to create specialists (they don't "just happen").

Different types of specialists become available as your technology advances, and some advances render certain specialists obsolete. A base of any size can have doctor or empath specialists, but a base must have Population 5 before it can create other types. To create a different specialist, 🖱 on a citizen's icon in the Base Control Screen.

The various types of specialist are:

- **Technician.** Technicians keep the base running at maximum efficiency, adding +3 to the Economy allotment per technician in the base. They become obsolete when you acquire Fusion Power technology, replaced by Engineers.

- **Doctor.** A healthy population is a happy population. Doctors increase Psych allotment at a base by +2 per doctor. Doctors are rendered obsolete by Centauri Meditation and are replaced by Empaths.

- **Librarian.** Librarians are an invaluable asset to research, providing +3 to Labs allotment per librarian. They require Planetary Networks, and are rendered obsolete by Mind/Machine Interface, replaced by Thinkers.

- **Engineer.** A corps of engineers can optimize all of a base's functions, yielding +3 to Economy and +2 to Labs per engineer. They are acquired along with Fusion Power technology, and they never become obsolete.

- **Empath.** Empaths have actually learned to use the psi potential of their brains, providing +2 to both Economy and Psych per empath. They require Centauri Meditation, and are rendered obsolete by Secrets of Alpha Centauri, replaced by Transcendi.

- **Thinker.** Thinkers have maximized the computational capacity of their brains and provide +1 Psych and +3 Labs per thinker. Thinkers require Mind/Machine Interface, and become obsolete with Secrets of Alpha Centauri, replaced by Transcendi.

- **Transcend.** The penultimate stage of human mental evolution, transcendi provide +2 to Economy, +2 to Psych, and +4 to Labs. They require Secrets of Alpha Centauri and they never become obsolete.

GOLDEN AGE

If a base of size three or greater has no Drones, and the number of Talents is equal to or greater than the number of Workers, that base enters a "Golden Age." For the duration of the Golden Age, the base's growth rate and energy production are both enhanced (equivalent to a +2 Growth, +1 Economy on the Social Engineering screen; see **Society Window**, p. 136). The Golden Age ends once there are more Workers than Talents, or if any Drones appear.

DRONE RIOTS

If the number of Drones in your population exceeds the number of Talents, the result is a **Drone Riot**, which shuts down the base's entire research and production capabilities. If left unchecked, rioting Drones start to destroy facilities, and may even cause a base to defect to a rival faction.

To end a Drone Riot, you can move military units into the base to act as police (the number of police needed is determined by your Social Engineering choices), adjust your Social Engineering to increase your Psych rating globally (see **Society Window**, p. 136), or create Specialists to increase it locally. To avoid Drone trouble in the long term, there are numerous facilities and Secret Projects, such as Recreation Commons and The Human Genome Project (see **Appendix 2**), that increase your Psych rating or suppress Drone activity.

When your faction grows very large, you come to a point where Drone production and inefficiency both accelerate dramatically. Beyond this point, extra Drones may appear due to the difficulty of managing a far-flung empire.

When you reach this threshold, your advisors remind you if you are about to found a base that sends you over the limit; you can choose to continue or abort. If you go past this point, make sure your social and economic choices are arranged to support it.

UNITS

Units are mobile teams created for military, engineering, trade, exploration or diplomatic purposes. There are land, sea and air units, many with special abilities. There are a multitude of different units that your faction can build as its technological abilities grow.

There are five vital statistics (*Movement Points, Attack Strength, Defense Strength, Reactor* and *Morale*) that determine how a unit rates in movement and combat.

- **Movement Points.** The number of squares the unit can enter each turn, assuming no external penalties or bonuses.

- **Attack Strength.** A measure of the unit's ability to overcome a defender.

- **Defense Strength.** A measure of the unit's ability to resist an attacker.

- **Reactor.** How much damage the unit can take before destruction. The reactor also affects the cost of a unit.

- **Morale.** A measure of the unit's discipline and experience. There are seven levels of Morale (see **Morale/Lifecycle**, p. 87), and it is the most important factor in Psi combat (see **Psi Combat**, p. 102).

FACILITIES

Facilities are major public improvements to a base. A base builds facilities to increase its efficiency, productivity and/or power. All facilities provide some useful benefit to a base, but not all benefits are necessary to a given base at a given time. Some facilities come with both benefits and costs and can do more harm than good if placed where they're not needed (punishment spheres, for example, eliminate Drone problems but reduce Labs production). Most facilities require an ongoing investment of energy credits to maintain, which is taken from energy allocated to Economy.

A complete list of **Facilities**, including their benefits and costs, can be found in **Appendix 2, p. 163**.

RELOCATE HEADQUARTERS

This build order (see **Build Orders, p. 67**) causes a new headquarters to be constructed in this base. You can only have one headquarters for you entire faction. When the new headquarters is completed, your previous one is disbanded. Headquarters provide essential coordination among the bases of your faction, which keeps inefficiency low. Inefficiency results from increasing distance from your headquarters, so it's usually good to maintain your headquarters near the center of your empire.

SECRET PROJECTS

Secret Projects are massive works requiring a great concentration of research effort and a very long time to complete. The good news is that they provide dramatic advantages to your faction.

Only one of each of the 32 Secret Projects can be built on Planet. The other faction leaders do anything they can to complete a Secret Project before you and claim its benefits for their faction. If a rival faction builds a Secret Project you're working on, you must transfer your research investment to some other Secret Project, or allocate it to new construction.

If a base with a Secret Project is ever completely destroyed, that project—and any ongoing benefits from it—are gone forever, for you and all other factions. If a base with a Secret Project is captured, that Secret Project—and any ongoing benefits from it—become the possession of the capturing faction.

A complete list of **Secret Projects** can be found in **Appendix 2, p. 170**.

STOCKPILE ENERGY

If you don't particularly need any new units or facilities from a base, but don't want to let its production capacity go to waste (or if your faction is strapped for cash) you can order your base to Stockpile Energy. This causes the base to immediately sell off every excess mineral it produces in exchange for energy credits, which are then deposited in your energy reserves.

BASE CONTROL SCREEN

The Base Control Screen is one of the main nerve centers of your society. Second only to the main map, this is where you'll do most of the actual "work" of playing *Sid Meier's Alpha Centauri*.

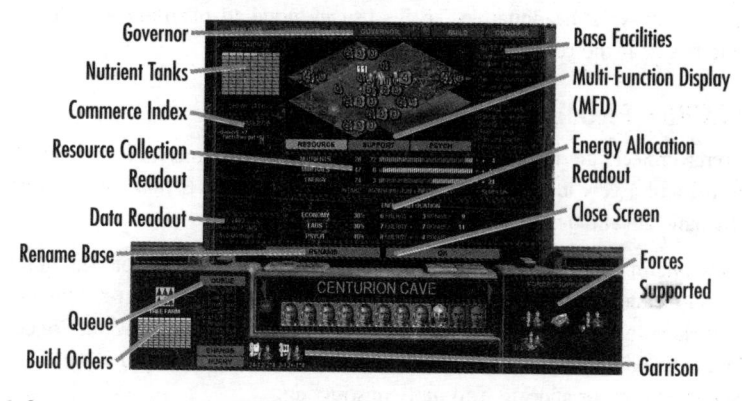

Labels (left side, top to bottom): Governor, Nutrient Tanks, Commerce Index, Resource Collection Readout, Data Readout, Rename Base, Queue, Build Orders

Labels (right side, top to bottom): Base Facilities, Multi-Function Display (MFD), Energy Allocation Readout, Close Screen, Forces Supported, Garrison

Information on each base, its citizens, resources, and production may be found on the **Base Control Screen.** There are several different ways to access this screen.

- 🖑 on the base you want to look at.

- Press [Enter] when the terrain square containing the base is highlighted or when a unit in the base is active.

- Double 🖑 on any base name on the Base Operations Status Screen (accessed via your HQ Menu, p. 110).

• 🖱 on the ZOOM button when selecting a base from the Locate Base screen (accessed via the **Map Menu**, p. 32).

A TOUR OF THE BASICS

The Base Control Screen allows you to control your base to a minuscule level, but if left alone the base can do a pretty good job of running itself. Most of the time, you'll be checking the Base Control Screen just to take a quick look at the current status of a base—what it's building, how its citizens are doing, and so forth. Below is a quick guide to reading the most important data from the Base Control Screen (you can also 🖱 on any part of the Base Control Screen for a short explanation of its function). Many of these readouts also provide advanced control functions, which are described below this section.

GOVERNOR

EXPLORE	DISCOVER	GOVERNOR	BUILD	CONQUER

This command bar allows you to automate management of the base, based on one of four broad priorities. 🖱 on any of the four choices (*Explore*, *Discover*, *Build* or *Conquer*; see **Governor**, p. 69) for specifically tailored development.

BUILD ORDERS

The Build Orders Window shows the base's current build orders, a graph indicating how far along it is (each square represents one mineral of cost—filled-in squares are saved minerals, empty ones remain to be collected), and an estimate of time to completion considering the base's current production rate. You can also 🖱 on the CHANGE button to establish new build orders (see **Production Readout**, p. 78).

RESOURCE MFD

The screen at the upper center of your Base Control Screen is a multi-function display (MFD): it can be set to display several different readouts, but the one we're interested in at the moment is the Resource MFD. This is

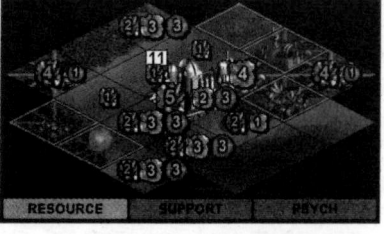

a map showing the territory controlled by the base and what resources each square is producing. (Squares outlined in white are under the control of a neighboring base.)

NUTRIENT TANKS

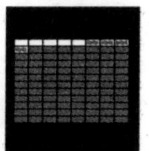

This graph shows how your base is growing. When your nutrient tanks fill up (all the squares are bright), the population of the base increases by one citizen and the nutrient tanks empty. Conversely, if your base isn't producing enough nutrients to support all its citizens, nutrients are drawn from the tanks. If the tanks empty and you still have a nutrient shortfall, you lose a citizen to starvation.

POPULATION

This readout shows every citizen in the base. If the number of red Drones is equal to or greater than the number of green Talents, watch out—that base is in danger of a Drone riot. (See **Drone Riots**, p. 63.)

BASE FACILITIES

This is simply a list of every facility and Secret Project currently built in the base.

BASE FACILITIES
Children's Creche
Recycling Tanks
Perimeter Defense
Recreation Commons
Energy Bank
Network Node
Biology Lab
Paradise Garden
Robotic Assembly
Quantum Converter
Hab Complex
Pressure Dome
Command Center

BASE CONTROL SCREEN —
SECTION BY SECTION

GOVERNOR

| EXPLORE | DISCOVER | GOVERNOR | BUILD | CONQUER |

If you'd rather not worry too much about the year-to-year operations of a particular base, you can put the Base Governor in charge, making it his responsibility to assign citizens to work and determine which squares to develop and what projects to undertake. If you don't like a decision that is made, you can always overrule it.

To activate the governor, ⊖ any of the five buttons at the top of the Base Control Screen. On lower difficulty levels, the governor is always active as the default.

The governor's priorities are set depending on which of the five options you select. (Once the governor is on, ⊖ on the active priority to turn the governor off.)

- **Default.** The governor pursues a strategy mixing growth and defense concerns. This is the automatic priority at difficulty levels where the governor defaults to "on." To activate the governor with default priorities, ⊖ on the GOVERNOR button until only that button is lit.

- EXPLORE. The base devotes itself primarily to producing units to explore new terrain. New colonization (colony pods) and population growth are also priorities.

- DISCOVER. The governor maximizes Labs output, seeking to optimize the speed of discovery of new technologies. It also emphasizes Secret Projects and probe teams for intelligence gathering.

- BUILD. The base disregards most external concerns, concentrating on its own growth, terraforming, and the creation of new facilities.

- CONQUER. The base goes on a war footing, producing primarily military units and facilities with specifically military applications (perimeter defense, command center).

MFD

The MFD (multi-function display) is located in the upper center portion of your Base Control Screen. It normally appears as a map of territory inside your base's production radius (this is the **Resource Screen**, below).

The MFD has three functions. To switch between functions, 🖰 on one of the three buttons below the MFD.

RESOURCE MFD

Central Base Square

Squares Under Production

Squares Not Under Production

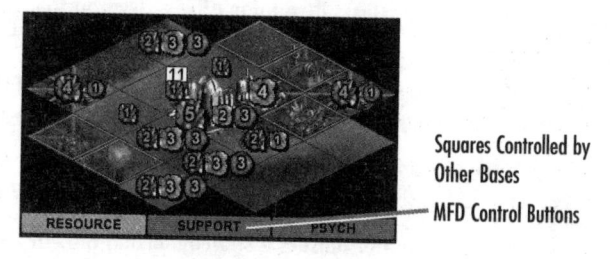

Squares Controlled by Other Bases

MFD Control Buttons

The resource MFD appears as a map of territory inside the base's production radius, showing terrain and any enhancements as they normally appear on the main map. Blacked-out squares are unexplored territory, and red-tinged squares with a white border are currently under production by a different base (yours or another faction's). Each square currently in production (i.e., with a worker assigned to it) displays the amount of each resource it is currently generating.

Icon	Icon Color	Resource
🟢	Green	Nutrients
🔵	Blue	Minerals
🟠	Orange	Energy

ASSIGNING CITIZENS TO WORK

Your Resource Screen is used to control your base's resource production.

If you 🖰 on any square currently under production, you reassign that square's worker to become a Specialist (see **Citizens**, p. 61). That square is immediately taken out of production.

If you 🖰 on any square not currently in production, the governor selects a Worker or Talent to begin working on that square. The governor selects a square to abandon in favor of the new square.

If you want to reassign a Worker from one specific square to another, 🖰 on the square you want to take out of production (to temporarily create a Specialist), then 🖰 on the new square to reassign that Worker to it. You can also drag and drop Workers from the population bar onto empty squares. Say, for example, that you suspect the Hive is getting ready to launch an invasion of your territory. This reassignment function allows you to order a crucial border base to live off nutrient tanks for a few turns while your Workers maximize mineral production to complete a Perimeter Defense without dipping into energy reserves.

If you 🖰 directly on the base square itself, the governor selects assignments for all available workers, with a view towards (a) meeting the base's current resource needs first, and (b) maximizing production (according to the governor's current priorities, if any).

71

SUPPORT MFD

This screen shows the location of all the base's units not located in the base itself. The Support Screen displays the entire world map, with the base appearing as a bright dot, and supported units as smaller dots.

PSYCH MFD

This screen displays a graphic readout of the citizens in the base and the effect of various factors on their attitude.

This graph contains up to five lines, each line cumulative with the ones above it. A line is only displayed if it's actually applicable to the base at the moment.

- **Unmodified.** Shows all citizens and their attitudes before other modifiers are taken into consideration.

- **Psych.** Shows attitudes modified by your energy allocation to Psych (see **Energy Allocation** p. 117), if any, cumulative with the above.

- **Facilities.** Shows attitudes modified by the base's facilities, if any, cumulative with the above.

- **Police.** Shows attitudes modified by any police units (see **Drone Riots**, p. 63) assigned to the base, cumulative with the above.

- **Secret Projects.** This line adds in the effects of any Secret Projects your faction has completed, cumulative with the above.

RESOURCE COLLECTION READOUT

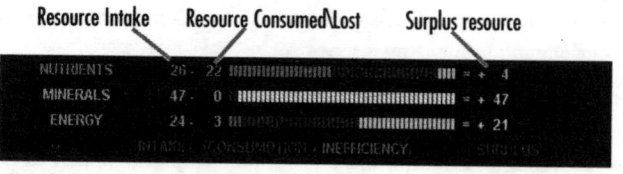

Resource Intake   Resource Consumed\Lost   Surplus resource

NUTRIENTS	26 - 22	= + 4
MINERALS	47 - 0	= + 47
ENERGY	24 - 3	= + 21

INTAKE - CONSUMPTION - INEFFICIENCY   SURPLUS

Located just below the main MFD, the Resource Collection Readout shows exactly how much of each resource your base is producing, and how each is being used.

- **Lost.** Red blocks are resources lost to inefficiency (see **Inefficiency**, p. 118).

- **Used.** Blocks to the **left** of the bar are being used for maintenance of units and facilities already completed (minerals) or to feed the population of the base (nutrients).

- **Surplus.** Blocks to the **right** of the bar are surplus, and are going to population growth (nutrients), project completion (minerals), or energy allocation (energy).

ENERGY ALLOCATION READOUT

This displays how energy collected at this base is allocated according to the priorities set in the Social Engineering Window (see **Energy Allocation**, p. 117).

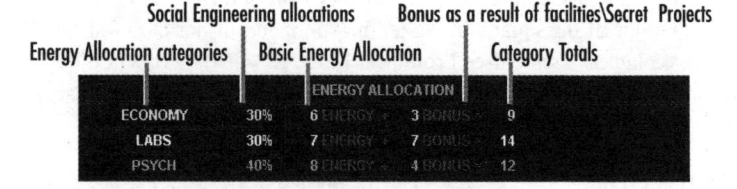

Social Engineering allocations — Bonus as a result of facilities\Secret Projects

Energy Allocation categories — Basic Energy Allocation — Category Totals

ENERGY ALLOCATION				
ECONOMY	30%	6 ENERGY +	3 BONUS =	9
LABS	30%	7 ENERGY +	7 BONUS =	14
PSYCH	40%	8 ENERGY +	4 BONUS =	12

- **Economy.** Energy allocated to Economy is used to maintain your base facilities; any surplus goes into your energy reserve.

- **Labs.** Energy allocated to Labs drives your research efforts.

- **Psych.** Energy allocated to Psych helps keep your people happy and productive.

73

DATA READOUT

This area (below the Resource Collection Readout) shows general useful information about the base.

- **Base Name.** The **arrow buttons** next to the base name allow you to cycle through the Base Control Screens of all your bases in alphabetical order. The right button cycles you forward through the alphabet, and the left button backwards.

Mission Year — Energy Reserves

Ecological Damage — Arrow Buttons

Base Name

M.Y. 2463
Energy: 33000
Eco-Damage: 0

QUEUE — CENTURION CAVE

- **Mission Year.** The current year according to Earth's Gregorian calendar.

- **Energy Reserves.** This is your faction's total energy reserves currently available for investment.

- **Ecological Damage.** If this number is higher than 0, there is a chance each turn that one of the squares in the production radius of this base will experience ecological disaster (see **Ecological Risks**, p. 54). The ecological damage number represents a percentage chance, per turn, of an ecological accident happening in the base's territory.

POPULATION

This bar below the data readout shows every citizen in your base. You can 🖰 on the citizen's icon to change Workers into Specialists, or Specialists into Workers or different sorts of Specialists. (See **Citizens**, p. 61.)

CONTROL BUTTONS

These buttons are located just beneath the Energy Allocation Readout.

- RENAME opens a dialogue box allowing you to change the name of the base.

- OK closes the Base Control Screen and resumes the current turn.

NUTRIENT TANKS

Each citizen in your base requires two nutrients per turn to survive. Any nutrients produced but not consumed (surplus) go into the nutrient tanks, whose status is shown in the upper left portion of the Base Control Screen. As the tanks fill up, the dark green squares turn bright.

Nutrients in Tanks
Projected Increase in Tanks Next Turn

Green squares with a white outline represent the projected increase in the tanks next turn, based on current production values. When the nutrient tanks are completely "full," your base increases its population by one, and the banks return to empty.

Likewise, if your base is not bringing in enough nutrients to support itself, the projected decrease in the tanks is shown by bright squares outlined in red. When the tanks are completely emptied, the base loses one unit of population to starvation. The base continues to lose one citizen per turn thereafter, until it reaches a population that can be supported by current nutrient production.

As your bases expand in size, the capacity of your nutrient tanks also expands. The larger your base, the more excess nutrients you need to increase its size further.

COMMERCE INDEX

Amount of Energy this Base Receives
from this Commerce each Year

Faction with whom you have Commerce

Treaty Status with that Faction

Amount of Energy they are Receiving
from the Commerce.

This screen records any ongoing trade between this base and any other faction. It displays the names of each faction you trade with, the diplomatic status of that faction (see **Diplomatic Relations**, p. 129), any energy coming in to that base, (i.e., +1) and energy from that base going to the faction being traded with. In general, the closer your ties with another faction, and the larger the faction, the more commerce increases.

BASE FACILITIES

This window (in the upper right of your Base Control Screen) lists all the facilities that have been built in the base.

Some Secret Projects provide a certain type of facility in each one of your bases. Such facilities appear dimmed in the Base Facilities window. Facilities received as part of a faction power (such as the Hive's Perimeter Defenses and the University's Network Nodes) also appear dimmed in this window. Facilities that are displayed with an *asterisk* (*) are obsolete or redundant. They can be scrapped without fear of losing any of your base's abilities or capacity.

BASE FACILITIES
Children's Creche
Recycling Tanks
Perimeter Defense
Recreation Commons
Energy Bank
Network Node
Biology Lab
Paradise Garden
Robotic Assembly
Quantum Converter
Hab Complex
Pressure Dome
Command Center

RECYCLE WINDOW

If you 🖱 on a facility in the Base Facilities Window, it brings up the Recycle Window. This allows you to demolish that facility and sell off the scrap for a few energy credits. When you call up the Recycle menu, you are given the options of:

- canceling

- consulting the Datalinks

- scrapping the facility

- scrapping all such facilities at all your bases

GARRISON

This bar displays pictures of each unit currently inside the base. Passing your cursor over a unit brings up its data in the Production Readout.

FORCES SUPPORTED

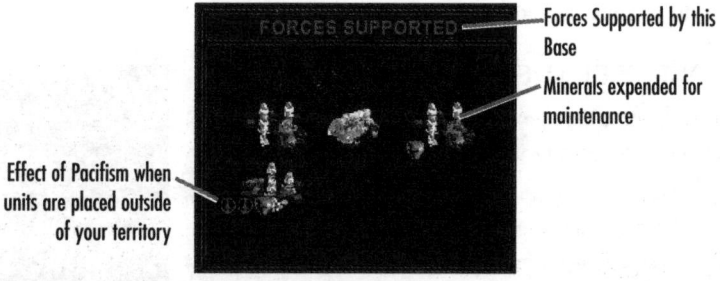

Forces Supported by this Base

Minerals expended for maintenance

Effect of Pacifism when units are placed outside of your territory

This window, in the bottom right corner of the screen, displays pictures of all the units anywhere on the surface of Planet currently supported by the base. Depending on your Social Engineering choices and the number of units a base supports, supported units may require a regular expenditure of minerals for maintenance, and military units stationed outside the base may also cause discontent among citizens. The number of units a base may support for free (if any) is determined by your support rating (see **Social Factors**, p. 141, and **Home Base, Support and Pacifism**, p. 89), while the number it can support before it starts to foment unrest is determined by your police rating (see **Social Factors**, p. 141).

Units that require minerals to be expended each turn for their support appear with a mineral icon next to them. Remote units which are causing unrest are indicated with a peace symbol.

🖰 on any unit in this display for a menu of orders that can be given to the unit. These options are:

- **Activate** (zooms to that unit, activates it, and closes the base screen).
- **Edit Unit** (appears only when scenario editor is activated; see **Appendix 4: Advanced Customization**, p. 206)
- **Sleep/Board Transport**
- **Hold**
- **Disband**
- **Order Unit to Come Home**

For more information on these commands, see **Action Menu**, p. 92.

BUILD ORDERS

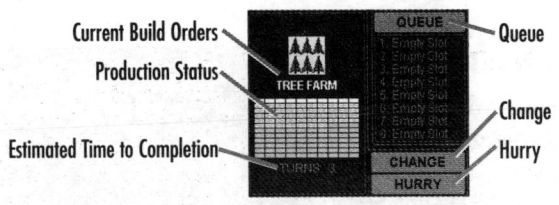

Current Build Orders

Production Status

Estimated Time to Completion

QUEUE — Queue

Change

Hurry

This extremely important section of the Base Control Screen is located in the lower left corner. This is where you track the base's progress in current build orders for units, facilities or Secret Projects, set new orders, or change orders when necessary. It consists of two windows.

CURRENT ORDERS

The window to the left displays a picture of the unit or the facility currently under construction.

The CHANGE button brings up the Production Readout (see **Production Readout,** below), from which you can select new orders.

The HURRY button allows you to expend extra energy credits to complete a project more quickly. The game displays the amount of energy necessary to complete the project, and you have the option of paying enough to complete the entire project on the next turn (if you have sufficient energy to do so), or of making a partial payment to speed up construction. You may only make one partial payment per turn.

QUEUE

The window to the right allows you to plan your development up to nine projects in advance.

If you 🖰 the QUEUE button, the Production Readout appears. Double-🖰 a selection from the readout to insert it at the top of the queue. You can 🖰 a currently occupied slot in the queue, then double-🖰 a selection in the Production Readout to insert the order at that slot (orders currently in the queue are not erased, they are just shifted down one slot each below the newly inserted order). For more information, see **Production Readout,** below.

PRODUCTION READOUT

This vitally important window can be accessed with the CHANGE or QUEUE buttons on the Base Control Screen. It includes a complete list of units, facilities and Secret Projects that your faction is currently capable of constructing. To order the con-

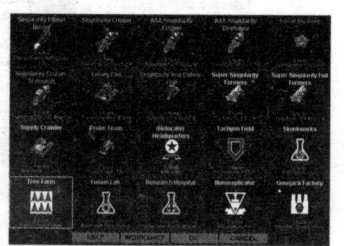

struction of a unit or facility, double-🖰 on its name to place it in production or into the queue.

There are a series of buttons along the bottom of the Production Readout. Some or all of the following buttons are available when you access the screen.

- HELP. Opens the Datalinks.

- WORKSHOP. Opens the Design Workshop (see **Designing Units**, p. 81).

- REPLACE. Replaces the highlighted project in the queue with a project you select.

- INSERT. Places new build orders in the queue at the point selected, without erasing any orders currently in the queue.

- DELETE. Deletes the selected project from the queue.

- CANCEL. Closes the Production Readout with no changes.

- OK. Accepts the current projects and closes the Production Readout.

SWITCHING PRODUCTION

If you decide to halt production on a Secret Project, unit or facility before it is complete and switch production to something new, you lose some of the minerals you have accrued towards the original project. The sole exception is switching from one Secret Project to another Secret Project, which does not forfeit any minerals.

You will *need* to switch production if a Secret Project you have been working on is completed by another faction first. If you stop a Secret Project, you can roll *all* of your investment into another Secret Project.

HOW MUCH DO YOU LOSE?

If you make any other kind of switch, you lose 50% of your investment after the first 10 minerals. This applies if you roll your investment from a Secret Project into anything but another Secret Project, or if you transfer your investment in a unit or facility to any other unit or facility.

The first 10 minerals that you invest transfer with no loss. All investment over 10 minerals is cut in half. For example, if you have invested 8 minerals, all 8 minerals transfer, with no loss. If you have invested 40 minerals, the first 10 transfer, as do half of the remaining 30: you transfer 25 (that is, 10 + 30/2) and you lose 15 (30/2).

If the transfer more than pays for the designated purchase, up to 10 of the remaining minerals are held over for your next production, with no additional loss. Anything over 10 minerals is lost completely. Continuing our example, where you have transferred 40 minerals (which are reduced to 25 minerals in the transfer): if you transfer those 25 minerals to a purchase that only requires 8 minerals, 10 of the remaining 17 minerals (25 - 8) are held over and can be applied to yet another purchase. The last 7 minerals are lost completely.

Up to 10 minerals can be held over between production orders even when orders are completed normally. For example, if you have a base producing 23 minerals, and it has 5 minerals left to create a unit, on the next turn it creates the unit (expending 5 minerals), carries 10 minerals over to the next production orders, and the final eight minerals are lost completely.

UNITS

Units are those elements of your faction—people and equipment—that actually go out upon the face of Planet and do things like fight, explore and discover.

At the most basic level there are three kinds of units in *Sid Meier's Alpha Centauri*—land, sea and air units. Land and sea units are basically self-explanatory—land units can only move on land squares, sea units on sea squares. Both types are subject to movement restrictions from fungus and other obstructions (see **How Terrain Affects Movement**, p. 44). A unit's *chassis* determines what kind of unit it is (see **Chassis**, p. 83).

Air units are a special case. They have no terrain restrictions at all, but most have a limited range. Air units carry only enough fuel for two turns of operations. The unit must replenish its fuel every other turn at a friendly base or airbase, or it runs out of fuel. The unit's movement is displayed as a split number, for example, 12/24. The first number is the amount of moves remaining this turn, and the second number is the total movement available over two turns. A yellow or red split number indicates that this aircraft should be heading for a nearby base to avoid the risk of a crash.

Choppers are air units, but they don't run out of fuel. Instead, they need ongoing maintenance when in regular use. If a chopper does not end its turn in a base or airbase, it takes a small amount of damage. (Damage is repaired, over time, when the chopper is at a base or airbase.) This damage weakens the chopper in combat, and can result in the chopper falling apart and crashing, if allowed to continue too long without repairs in a base or airbase.

DESIGNING UNITS

As you advance technologically, you are given the option of using units predesigned by your designers, or of designing your own units, using a fixed assortment of components. Custom-designed units allow you to specifically tailor units to your personal mission needs and also make full use of some of the more exotic special abilities. New components are discovered in conjunction with many technology advances (see **Special Abilities Table**, p. 183). For example, High Energy Chemistry allows you to build with plasma steel armor and nerve gas pods.

To design a new unit, press ⒰, or access the Design Workshop Screen from the HQ menu or the Production Readout.

Units are made up of up to six components:

- Chassis
- Armament
- Armor
- Reactor
- Special Abilities (up to two)

PROTOTYPES

Any time you order construction of a unit with untried components, that unit is a prototype. If you have already built a laser crawler and an impact rover, your first laser rover (which consists entirely of components found in the previous units) would not require a prototype. But if you discovered the missile launcher and decided to build a missile rover, the new missile launcher component would make your first missile rover a prototype.

Prototypes require a great deal of research and development. Therefore, a prototype costs 50% more minerals to complete than subsequent units of this type will. On the upside, all prototype units get a +1 to morale, since new technologies are usually put in the care of elite forces. Note that the Spartans do not have to prototype new units due to their expertise with military hardware.

OBSOLETE UNITS

As new versions of components are researched, old ones become obsolete. Units with obsolete components disappear from your Production Readout and are replaced by the newer models. You can also declare units of a given kind obsolete from the Design Workshop.

UPGRADES

When an old unit becomes obsolete, you don't have to junk it or let it wheeze around. When you discover a new version of a component, you are given the option of upgrading all the units that discovery has made obsolete. You must pay an energy charge for each obsolete unit in your possession in order to upgrade them. If you don't want to spend the energy to upgrade all your units of a given sort at once, you can also upgrade one at a time, using the Upgrade command—Ctrl Shift U on the Action menu (see p. 92). (Note that you can also disband a unit at a base, and receive half its original cost in minerals.)

CHASSIS

The Chassis of the unit determines two vital characteristics: whether the unit is a land, sea or air unit; and its basic movement rate (see Movement, p. 90).

A complete list of Chassis types and their associated values can be found in the Units Table, p. 175.

WEAPON

The unit's weapon type determines its offensive firepower. A list of armaments and their associated values appears on the Armament Table, p. 177.

An important special weapon is the Psi attack, described under Psi Combat, p. 102.

Non-combat units (colony pods, terraformers, and the like) can take unique abilities in their weapon slot—for example, transport modules, colony modules or probe team equipment.

ARMOR

A unit's armor determines its basic defense strength. A unit is not required to have armor—even unarmored units get a small intrinsic defense strength.

A complete list of armor types and their associated values appears on the Defenses Table, p. 180.

REACTOR

Reactor Power determines how much damage the unit can actually take before it's destroyed. Also, more advanced reactors actually reduce the costs of units. A complete list of reactors with associated values appears on the Reactors Table, p. 182.

SPECIAL ABILITIES

You can also endow your units with *special abilities* to fulfill specific tactical needs. Some are geared towards attack, some to defense, and some are more esoteric. If, for example, the Gaians are attacking your faction with an invasion force of mind worms, you might want to counter with a force of units equipped with the Hypnotic Trance special ability, which gives the units a +50% defensive bonus against psi attacks. In the early stages of the game you can have no more than one special ability per unit type, but you acquire the ability to mount two special abilities on the same unit with the discovery of Neural Grafting.

A complete list of special abilities, with descriptions, can be found on the **Special Abilities Table, p. 183.**

CUSTOM UNITS

If you decide to build your own units to use in addition to the pre-designed units, you should know that the cost factors (given in **Appendix 2**) are not simply additive. The cost for a custom unit with many advanced features is far above the sum of its component prices. In fact, often if you take a "super unit" and tone down just one or two components a notch or two, you will find that you can now afford two or more of the slightly more modest units for the same price you'd have paid for a single super unit. Consider designing two different types of units which complement each others' weaknesses rather than trying for one unit with no weaknesses. Advanced reactors make the unit more efficient and actually reduce its cost, so an advanced reactor can make more sophisticated units more affordable.

Many special abilities are, for obvious reasons, unavailable on units of a certain type. Aircraft, for example, cannot mount heavy artillery, while combat units cannot mount a heavy transport module.

CHAPTER 4

BUILDING UNITS

Custom-designed units can be created in the Design Workshop, which can be accessed with ⓤ, or from the HQ menu or the Production Readout.

You can get a head start in designing the type of unit you want by either selecting a specific unit to modify, or by using a vehicle preset.

Specific unit designs are displayed in the long bar at the bottom of the screen. This bar contains all the unit types currently designed and in production, and can be scrolled using the arrow buttons at either end of the bar. Units which are obsolete to your faction, but still in production, are marked "obs." Placing your cursor over any of the units in the bar displays information about that unit in the lower left window. 🖱 on the unit to place it in the design screen for modification.

85

VEHICLE PRESETS

Vehicle presets are up-to-date versions of various vehicle types in a number of categories:

- **Garrison.** Defensive units designed to protect bases and fortifications.

- **Infantry.** General-purpose combat units particularly useful for attacking bases.

- **Artillery.** Units with long-range fire capability (see **Artillery Combat**, p. 100).

- **Tank.** Mobile units useful for attacks in open terrain.

- **Scout.** Lightly armored, very fast units.

COLONIZING PLANET

- **Naval.** Combat ships.

- **Transport.** Non-combat ships designed to carry goods or personnel.

- **Air Assault.** Heavy bombers.

- **Air Defense.** Fighters designed to intercept and engage other aircraft.

- **Chopper.** Rotary-wing aircraft.

- **Missile.** One-use air units—once they hit their target, they are destroyed.

- **Buster.** Missile units capable of annihilating bases and the surrounding terrain.

- **Paradrop.** Units capable of performing airdrops and orbital insertions (see **Drop Pods,** p. 91).

- **Amphibious.** Units capable of attacking directly from ship to shore, or attacking sea bases from land.

86 DESIGN WORKSHOP

Once you've chosen a starting point, you can make the specific modifications you desire. The large round window shows the unit in development, its current stats and a working name based on its components. It also displays the unit's cost, and a prototype cost if a prototype is necessary. This window is surrounded by six readouts showing the six component slots. 🖰 on a slot to select the component you want for your custom unit.

Control Buttons. There are seven control buttons below the Design Window. They are:

- APPLY. If a new unit type has been created, it's placed in your Production Readout.

- DONE. Exits the Design Window. If a new unit type has been created, it is placed in your Production Readout.

- RENAME. Allows you to give the unit type a name other than its working designation.

- OBSOLETE. The unit type is removed from your Production Readout.

- UPGRADE. Upgrades all units of this type to a superior design, if one is available.

- CANCEL. Closes the Design Window with no changes.

- RETIRE. Disbands all units of this type, and removes the unit type from your Production Readout.

BASIC UNIT TYPES

Certain unit types begin the game already designed and prototyped:

- Colony Pod

- Basic Formers and Sea Formers (Super Formers can be modified)

- Scout Patrol

- Transport Foil and Supply Crawler

- Probe Team

- Native life-forms—mind worms, Isles of the Deep, Locusts of Chiron

- Alien Artifact (cannot be built, must be found)

- *Unity* units—*Unity* Rover, *Unity* Scout Chopper, *Unity* Foil (cannot be built, must be found)

As your technology advances you may want to design newer, more powerful units to fulfill these roles.

MORALE/LIFECYCLE

One of the most important aspects of any given unit is its morale—its overall discipline and experience. There are several levels of morale. Morale for native life-forms (mind worms, Isles of the Deep and Locusts of Chiron) is called life-cycle level, since a native unit's morale reflects not only the experience of its human handlers, but also its physical maturity.

Morale	Native Lifecycle
Very Green	Hatchling
Green	Larval Mass
Disciplined	Pre-Boil
Hardened	Boil
Veteran	Mature Boil
Commando	Great Boil
Elite	Demon Boil

The importance of morale in combat cannot be overstated. Each level of morale gives a +12.5% bonus to the unit, in both offensive and defensive combat.

The most common manner in which a unit's morale is increased is for it to survive combat and be promoted, but there are other ways to increase morale of both individual units and of your military in general. These include:

- **Monoliths** have been known to increase the morale of individual units (see *Unity* Pods and Monoliths, p. 42).

- **Base Facilities** can increase the morale of units made at that base. Command Centers provide +2 to land units, Naval Yards provide +2 to sea units, Aerospace Complexes provide +2 to air units, and Bio-enhancement Centers provide +2 to all units. Facilities provide morale bonuses only to units made after the facility's completion; they do nothing for units already existing at the time they're built.

  Several base facilities also increase the lifecycle of any native units bred. The following confer +1 lifecycle bonus: Biology Lab, Centauri Preserve and Temple of Planet.

- **Secret Projects**

- **Social Engineering** (see Social Factors, p. 141)

HOME BASE, SUPPORT AND PACIFISM

The base that builds a unit is that unit's home base. Units taken over by probe teams, or wild mind worms "tamed" by your faction, become the responsibility of the base geographically closest to the spot where the unit was acquired by your faction. A few units, such as those acquired far away from any base, do not require a home base at all.

You may change a unit's home base by moving that unit to a new base and selecting Set Home Base ([Ctrl][H]) from the Action menu. That base now supports the unit. The home base must pay the unit's support cost, if any.

A support cost represents the cost of keeping a unit equipped and staffed. The cost for a given unit may be zero or one mineral per turn (as determined by your faction's support rating; see **Social Factors**, p. 141). It is subtracted from minerals collected at the home base. If you find that a base cannot build new orders as quickly as it used to, it's often the result of too many minerals used for support of existing units. In this case, try disbanding old or obsolete units (See **Design Workshop**, p. 86) so more minerals can go towards new production.

If your faction has a Police rating less than 2 (see **Social Factors**, p. 141), it is considered to be *Pacifist*. When a pacifist faction creates a unit and stations it anywhere outside its own territory (see **Territory**, p. 131), additional drones (see **Citizens**, p. 61) are created at the unit's home base (representing social discord). On the base screen, the Forces Supported Readout shows the effects of pacifism as a peace symbol, one for each Worker that has become a Drone because of a unit outside its territory.

MOVEMENT

There's more to getting your units where they need to go than just pushing them around the map. Moving a unit is an operation all to itself, and there are several essential principles you must keep in mind (plus a couple of exotic options that you can try).

In the absence of external bonuses or penalties to movement (see **How Terrain Affects Movement**, p. 45), a unit can move a number of squares equal to its movement rating. Land units can move only from one land square to another, and sea units can only enter sea squares.

ZONES OF CONTROL

Bases and land and air units exert a "zone of control" that restricts movement in their immediate vicinity, reflecting the difficulty of moving with an enemy nearby. A zone of control affects the eight squares immediately adjacent to a base or unit.

A zone of control has no effect on units of the same faction, units of factions sharing a Pact of Brotherhood, sea units, air units, or probe teams.

RESTRICTIONS TO MOVEMENT

A unit cannot move directly from one enemy zone of control to another. A unit can enter or exit an enemy zone of control freely as long as both squares are *not* enemy controlled.

A unit can always move into a base square, or into a square containing at least one friendly unit, regardless of zones of control.

Probe team units always ignore zones of control.

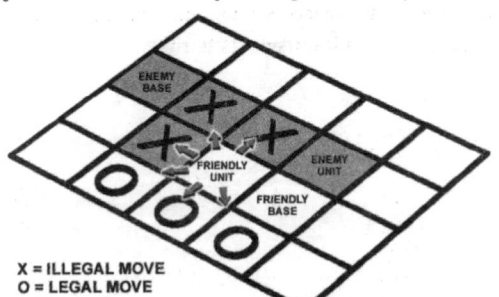

X = ILLEGAL MOVE
O = LEGAL MOVE

An advanced special ability—the Cloaking Device—makes a unit effectively invisible to the enemy, thereby allowing it to ignore zones of control.

DROP PODS

Drop Pods are a special ability component that allows units to make airdrops or orbital insertions. Discovery of Mind/Machine Interface allows construction of Drop Pods. Any unit with Drop Pods may make airdrops. Once you discover Graviton Theory or build the Space Elevator Secret Project, any unit with Drop Pods may make an orbital insertion.

To perform an airdrop or orbital insertion, the Drop Pod unit must begin in a friendly base or airbase, and may not have moved already this turn. At the drop command, ⌐I⌐, a parachute icon appears and you can 🖱 the destination square. The destination square may be up to 8 squares away and can not contain enemy units or bases. The Drop Pod unit moves instantly from the start square to the destination square. Units take damage from airdrops—20% damage, or 26% if the unit has a singularity reactor.

If a unit tries to drop and then attack on the same turn, it receives a 50% penalty to attack strength.

Orbital insertions are executed identically, but the drop can be made anywhere on Planet.

An interceptor unit (see **Air Combat**, p. 101) stationed in a base within two squares of the drop point prevents an air drop to that location.

ACTION MENU

The Action menu contains all the commands that you can give your units
(except for Terraforming commands, which are found on the **Terraform Menu**,
p. 46). Some of these options only appear if your unit is capable of performing that action at the moment (for example, a combat unit that is not in a
base will not see the Obliterate Base option).

CONSTRUCT BASE [B]

This command can only be carried out by a colony pod. The pod transforms
itself into a new base at its current location (if its current square is one on
which a base can be built; see **Resources**, p. 36).

OBLITERATE BASE [B]

This command can only be carried out by a combat unit (any unit with offensive armament) inside a base. It completely obliterates that base, putting all
the citizens to death and leaving nothing but bare terrain. This is an atrocity
(see **Atrocities**, p. 106), and results in severe repercussions from other faction
leaders. (Note that obliterating a base which you just conquered is considered
a worse atrocity than destroying one you built yourself—the other factions are
distinctly upset by any hint of "factional cleansing" on Planet.)

LONG RANGE FIRE [F]

Some units (notably artillery) can fire up to two squares away. To conduct long
range fire, select this command (your cursor changes to a target symbol) and
🖰 on the square you wish to attack. If there are enemy units in the target
square you attack those units, and if there are no enemy units you attack
enemy terrain enhancements.

AIR DROP [I]

Orders a unit equipped with a Drop Pod to make an air drop or orbital insertion. When you select this action, your cursor changes to a parachute icon, and

you can select a square to drop to. See **Drop Pods**, p. 91, for a full explanation of air drops.

PSI GATE [Shift][I]

Orders a unit to teleport from any base equipped with a Psi Gate facility to any other of your bases so equipped. When you use this command a window appears displaying all available destinations. Select the desired destination to complete the movement.

CONVOY RESOURCES [O]

Orders a supply unit to deliver resources. It has two distinct functions:

- If the supply unit is outside a base, it delivers available resources from its square to its home base each turn. Choosing this command brings up a menu from which you select the resources you wish to convoy. The unit cannot deliver resources from a square already being worked by a base's citizens.

- If the unit is within a base, it convoys resources *from* its home base to its current location every turn.

DESTROY ENHANCEMENTS [D]

Orders a combat unit or former to attack and destroy any enhancements in the square it currently occupies.

DISBAND UNIT [Shift][D]

Permanently destroys a unit, taking it completely out of play. If done at a base, you get 50% of the original construction cost back. If the unit is outside a base, you get the option to "Self Destruct," which violently destroys the unit while also damaging units in adjacent squares.

AUTOMATE UNIT [Shift][A]

The unit's commander determines the course of action.

EXPLORE AUTOMATICALLY [/]

The unit, under its commander's discretion, seeks out and explores uncharted terrain.

PATROL [P]

This orders a unit to patrol back and forth between its current location and a second square you select. Use this command, then 🖱 on the second square.

DESIGNATE BOMBING RUN [B]

This order designates an enemy base as a target for routine air attacks. The unit attacks the base you select, returns to the nearest friendly base, repairs its damage, then attacks again. The unit continues until its orders change or it is destroyed.

GO TO BASE/SET AUTOFORWARD ROUTE [G]

94

Select "go to base" to issue orders to a unit you want to move towards a particular base. The unit goes to any of your bases by the most direct route possible (if it can't actually reach the base it goes to the closest square). Selecting this command brings up dialogue from which you select a destination.

When in view mode (see **Map Menu**, p. 32) and centered on a base, pressing [G] allows you to set an autoforward route. This option commands any unit without orders in one base to head to another that you select, setting up a central rallying point for your troops. You may set autoforward routes for any kind of unit.

GROUP GO TO [J]

This orders an entire group to go to a location you select (see **Assemble Group**, facing page). Use mouse movement (see **Mouse Movement**, p. 21) to 🖱 and drag to the group's final destination, then use this command before releasing. The line showing the proposed route to the destination changes from green to yellow. If you have not assembled a group, all units in the current square are moved.

ASSEMBLE GROUP [Shift][J]

Orders your units to converge on the square with the active unit. When you use the assemble group command, you see a window that allows you to customize your group, with options to:

• Exclude units further than two squares away

• Exclude units with hold and sentry orders

• Exclude automated and patrol units

• Exclude ground, sea, air, offensive combat, defensive combat, terraformer, or probe team units.

• Exclude other units

Once you've established the parameters of your group, 🖰 ASSEMBLE AT CURSOR to assemble the group at a spot you then select, CANCEL GROUP to cancel all group orders, CANCEL to exit the screen without taking action, or OK to assemble the group on the square with the active unit.

GO TO HOME BASE [Shift][G]

The unit returns to its home base by the most direct route possible.

SET HOME BASE [Ctrl][H]

If the active unit is in a base square, this command reassigns the unit to be supported by that base. This command does not appear if the unit is not in a base. See **Home Base, Support and Pacifism**, p. 89, for more on home bases.

ACTIVATE (MOVE NOW) [A]

Makes the unit under the cursor the active unit (see **Active Units**, p. 22). A unit that has already exhausted all its movement points can still be activated with this command, and given orders that don't involve further movement in the current turn.

WAIT (MOVE LATER) [W]

This unit is skipped for now, but is re-activated again before the end of the turn.

UNLOAD TRANSPORT [Shift][U]

Each unit being carried by a transport activates in turn, and may be moved ashore.

UPGRADE UNIT [Ctrl][U]

This command only works if the unit can be upgraded (see **Upgrades**, p. 82). At the command to upgrade the unit, you are told how much the upgrade costs, and given the option of canceling or continuing. If more than one possible upgrade is available, you are asked to choose.

DESIGNATE DEFENDER [Ctrl][D]

Allows you to select the unit in a stack that defends first in the event of an attack on that square. Otherwise, the computer automatically selects the unit with the highest defense strength as the defender. This command is useful if you don't want your best unit in a stack to take the brunt of the attack, preferring to keep it in reserve for a counterattack.

SENTRY/BOARD TRANSPORT [L]

The unit stands down to repair itself, while posting sentries and maintaining a state of readiness. It stays in position and does not reactivate unless:

• it repairs itself to the maximum it can achieve under current field conditions

• an enemy unit enters an adjacent square

• it is attacked by artillery

If used in a base, this command causes the unit to automatically board any transport that has room for it.

PLACE UNIT ON ALERT (Shift)(L)

Orders a unit to hold in the current square until an enemy unit comes within its movement range, then attack automatically. Air interceptor units automatically attack air units, bomber units attack land and sea units, and naval units attack naval units and transports. Land units attack adjacent land units.

HOLD 10 TURNS (Shift)(H)

The unit holds its current position for 10 turns, then activates.

HOLD THIS POSITION (H)

The unit stays in its current position indefinitely. You must activate it directly to change its orders.

SKIP TURN (Spacebar)

Ends the current turn for that unit.

97

COMBAT

At some point, even for the most peaceful and enlightened faction, armed conflict becomes inevitable. And, of course, if your faction is neither peaceful nor enlightened—if you actually like going out and beating up on the enemy—then armed conflict is not just inevitable, but essential.

Combat occurs when a unit tries to enter a square containing an enemy base or unit. (Probe teams are the exception here—their options are much more subtle. See **Probe Teams**, p. 133.)

Combat is decided by totaling the attacker's strength and the defender's strength. The probability of either side doing damage is equal to that side's portion of their combined strengths. (For example, if the attacker has an attack strength of 10 and the defender a defense strength of 20, the attacker only damages the defender once, on average, for every two times the defender damages the attacker.) This process of assessing damage repeats until either the attacker or defender is destroyed (the exceptions are artillery, p. 100, and disengage, below). It is entirely possible for the winner of a battle to come out severely damaged.

STACKED DEFENDERS

If a unit attacks a square containing multiple defending units, the unit with the highest defense acts as the defender (unless you have designated another unit in the stack as the defender; see **Action Menu**, p. 92). If the defender is defeated, and the square is not a base or bunker square, the rest of the combat units in that square take collateral damage (that is, they each take a certain amount of damage, determined by the reactor of the attacking unit).

Non-combat units in a stack are destroyed along with the last combat unit in the square.

DISENGAGEMENT

In combats where the defending unit is faster than the attacker (i.e., the defender has at least one more movement point than the other), the faster unit can disengage if the battle is going against it. When a unit disengages, it simply moves one square away from the attacker. This assumes, of course, that the square into which the unit is retreating is not blocked by impassable terrain or an enemy zone of control (see **Zones of Control**, p. 90). A faster defender automatically disengages when it has received 50% damage.

If the attacker has the ECM Jammer special ability, the defending unit can't disengage from combat, even if faster. Also, if the defender attacked in its immediately preceding turn, it may not disengage under any circumstance.

COMBAT MODIFIERS

In addition to the strength of the units themselves, there are also external factors that can affect the outcome of combat. These take the form of percentage bonuses or penalties to the unit's base score. For example, if a defending unit has a normal defensive strength of 20, a +15% bonus would give it an effective strength of 23.

SPECIAL ABILITIES

Many unit special abilities convey a bonus in combat (or inflict a penalty on the enemy). See the list in **Appendix 2, p. 183.**

TERRAIN

There are several occasions where terrain directly affects the odds in combat.

• Artillery units (see **Artillery Combat,** next page) get a +25% bonus per level of altitude if they are at a higher altitude than their targets.

• Mobile units in smooth or rolling terrain get a +25% offensive bonus, reflecting their ability to make the most of their agility.

• Any units in smooth or rolling terrain get a +50% defensive bonus against artillery attacks.

• A unit in rocky terrain gets a +50% defensive bonus.

• A unit in xenofungus gets a +50% defensive bonus, unless being attacked by a native life unit (in which case the attacker gets a +50% offensive bonus), or by a faction that has built the Pholus Mutagen Secret Project.

HASTY ASSAULT

Each time a land unit attacks, it drains one full movement point from the unit's total move. If you have less than one full movement point remaining when you attack, that is considered a *hasty assault*, and it puts you at a serious disadvantage. If you have 2/3 of a movement point remaining, you lose 33% of your attack strength, and if you have only 1/3 of a movement point remaining, your penalty is 66%. (Movement status does not affect defensive strength.)

A hasty assault always drains any fractional movement you have remaining.

Sea units, air units and mind worms do not suffer the negative consequences of making a hasty assault.

BUNKERS AND BASES

Bunkers and bases offer a +25% defensive bonus to units within them. They also eliminate the effects of collateral damage. However, infantry gets a +25% bonus when attacking a base.

SENSORS

Units within 2 squares of a friendly Sensor Array (see **Terraform Menu**, p. 46) get a +25% defensive bonus.

AIRDROPS AND ORBITAL INSERTIONS

Drop units (see **Drop Pods**, p. 91) get a -50% penalty if they attack on the same turn in which they make the drop.

NON-COMBAT UNITS

Unarmed units get -50% penalty defending against combat units. A unit is considered "non-combat" if it has no weapon and no armor, so a former unit with plasma steel armor does not get the non-combat penalty when attacked.

ARTILLERY COMBAT

Naval units and units with the artillery special ability are able to use the Long Range Fire ([F]) command (see **Action Menu**, p. 92).

Unlike most combat, artillery combat (combat using the Long Range Fire command) does not continue until a unit is destroyed. Attack and defense strengths of the units are compared only once, and (if the defender loses the single round of combat) a point of damage is assessed against the defender. This reflects the nature of artillery combat, which is basically firing blind to harass and weaken the enemy. Note that land units can never be completely destroyed by artillery fire, and units in a base or bunker can never be damaged more than 50%, although repeated barrages will keep them from repairing damage. Targeting a square with no units for an artillery barrage actually attacks any terrain enhancments in the square.

ARTILLERY DUELS

An exception to this rule occurs when one artillery unit attacks another. In this case an **artillery duel** occurs, as each unit focuses its fire on the other. Artillery duels are to the death, just like most other combats, but they utilize attack strengths only.

ARTILLERY COMBAT MODIFIERS

- Artillery units get a +25% bonus for each level of altitude (see **Energy (Elevation)**, p. 38) they are above the target.

- Land-based artillery gets a +50% bonus when attacking naval units.

- A unit in smooth or rolling terrain gets a +50% defensive bonus against artillery attacks to represent maneuverability as a defensive measure against artillery.

AIR COMBAT

There are two basic types of aircraft, bombers and interceptors. Bombers may only attack bases and surface units; they cannot attack air units. Interceptors can attack other air units, but are at a penalty when attacking surface targets. Specifically, interceptors attack other air units at twice their normal offensive power, but land and sea targets at only half normal strength. (Combat between two interceptors is at normal odds.) Any unit can attack a chopper.

To attack needlejets in flight (i.e., anywhere outside of a base or an airbase), a unit must have the Air Superiority special ability . Air units at bases and airbases are considered to be "on the runway," and can be attacked by any unit.

Missiles are a special kind of air unit. They are one-shot "fire and forget" weapons. Missiles are always destroyed after an attack, even if they win.

Air units can attempt to destroy enemy terrain enhancements by flying over the enhancement and using the Destroy Improvement command (see **Action Menu**, p. 92).

The Designate Bombing Run and On Alert commands (see **Action Menu, p. 92**) can also be used to automate air combat.

AIR COMBAT MODIFIERS

Air units receiving an artillery strike get a +100% bonus to defense strength. (An artillery unit must have the Air Superiority special ability to attack air units.)

NAVAL COMBAT

Sea units can attack normally against other sea units and sea bases. Attacks against bases and units on shore are handled as artillery strikes. (See **Artillery Combat, p. 100**) A sea unit does not have to have the artillery special ability to attack adjacent coastal squares.

NAVAL COMBAT MODIFIERS

Ships in a base square are considered to be "in port," and defend at a -50% penalty against land and air units (for a net penalty of -25%, after the +25% defensive bonus for being in a base is factored in). Against other naval vessels, ships in port fight as normal.

PSI COMBAT

Psi combat is conducted by the native life forms of Planet (mind worms, Isles of the Deep, Locusts of Chiron) and by certain advanced technological units. Psi combat seeks to turn the enemy's own minds against them, inducing horrible hallucinations and phobias, which cripple the enemy's ability to defend itself, and may even induce self-destructive behavior.

Morale modifies the basic factors used for psi combat, such as weapon and armor strength. Thus an Isle of the Deep of Mature Boil status (morale level 5) would usually overrun a green unit (morale level 2), but would probably find itself overmatched against a commando unit (morale level 6). Again, normal weapon and defense strengths are completely irrelevant to psi combat—a tiny *Unity* rover of Hardened status would be more likely to survive than a singularity cruiser of Disciplined status.

PSI COMBAT MODIFIERS

- The attacking unit gets a 3-to-2 advantage in psi combat when the defending unit is a land unit.

- Units may install the special abilities of Hypnotic Trance (discovered with Secrets of the Human Brain) and Empath Song (discovered with Centauri Empathy), which each provide +50% in psi combat.

- A faction's units gain a +10% psi attack bonus for each positive level of their Planet rating (see **Social Factors**, p. 141). Factions with negative Planet ratings receive an equivalent penalty.

- The Neural Amplifier Secret Project gives its faction a +50% psi defense bonus. The Dream Twister Secret Project grants a +50% psi attack bonus.

DAMAGE

When a unit takes damage, the colored bar graph located just above and to the left shows how badly it's been hurt. As the bar descends, it also changes color from green to yellow to red. When the bar is completely exhausted, the unit is destroyed.

Damage Bar

As surface units take damage, their movement rates decline. This reduces the maximum move of vehicles with a move of more than one, and also makes it more difficult for vehicles to enter fungus squares.

Units repair damage by remaining undisturbed for a turn. To skip a unit's turn, press (Spacebar). If they move or come under fire, they do not repair that turn. No unit may repair itself to better than 20% damage (80% normal strength) using field repairs, unless your faction possesses the Nano Factory Secret Project. The Sentry command can streamline the field repair process, requiring much less of your attention ([L]; see **Action Menu**, p. 92). In a base, several facilities can repair an undisturbed unit in one turn:

- A Command Center repairs land units in one turn

- A Naval Yard repairs naval units in one turn

- An Aerospace Complex repairs air units in one turn

- A Biology Lab repairs native units in one turn

Units repair at least 10% of their damage each turn, modified as follows:

- +10% in friendly territory

- +10% if air unit at airbase

- +10% if land unit in bunker

- +10% if in a base

- x2 rate if a land unit is on board a Transport with a Repair Bay

- +100% if the controlling faction owns the Nano Factory Secret Project.

104 BASES AND FACILITIES

Numerous base facilities affect combat, either directly or indirectly.

All units inside a base get a +25% bonus to their defense, and units in bases do not take collateral damage (see **Damage**, p. 103). You can designate a unit to act as the primary defender (using Ctrl D, or the Designate Defender command in the Action menu), or the game automatically defends with the strongest defensive unit in the base.

When the last base defender is eliminated in combat, the base population goes down. This population loss can be avoided by building a Perimeter Defense facility in the base.

Building a Perimeter Defense or Tachyon Field doubles the defense strengths of all the units in the base. Building both of these facilities triples defense strengths.

Units in a headquarters base automatically gain +1 Morale when defending.

CONQUEST AND ANNIHILATION

When all the combat units defending a base are destroyed (including naval units "in port" and air units "on the strip") the base can be entered by an attacking unit, causing the base to pass into the control of the attacking faction. (If a wild native life unit is attacking an undefended base, the native life form devours one citizen from the base, then dissipates.)

If the base population is reduced to zero in combat, the base ceases to exist. Any Secret Projects within it are lost forever, to all factions. Land units within the base at the time of its destruction are left intact; sea and air units are destroyed.

Conquering a base destroys a random number of the base's facilities.

ATTACKING ENHANCEMENTS

You can destroy enhancements in an undefended square, including roads, farms and other enhancements, by moving a unit onto that square and executing the Destroy Enhancement command (D).You can destroy only one enhancement per unit per turn. In squares with multiple enhancements you are prompted to choose the one to destroy.

AIR, COASTAL AND ARTILLERY BOMBARDMENTS

You can attack enhancements in undefended squares using artillery, aerial bombing runs, or coastal bombardment. However, unlike a direct attack, such actions are not guaranteed to be successful—they have a certain percentage chance of actually hitting something significant. Air units attack enhancements with a 75% success rate, artillery attacks with a 50% success rate, and missiles always hit their targets. If you are successful bombarding a square using artillery, a random enhancement is destroyed. If you attack using aerial bombardment, you choose the enhancement to destroy.

Artillery and naval bombardment attacks are made using Long Range Fire (see **Action Menu**, p. 92). Air attacks are made by moving into the square and using the D (Destroy Enhancement) command.

ATROCITIES

Atrocities are crimes against humanity. They always draw a radical response from the other faction leaders, ranging from trade sanctions to a war of extermination against your faction. But, if a majority of the Planetary Council votes to repeal the U.N. Charter (see **Planetary Council**, p. 132), then these actions no longer count as atrocities.

Atrocities include:

- **Planet Buster.** Any use of the base-destroying planet buster missile. This will cause swift and harsh reaction from all factions.

- **Nerve Gas.** Activating the nerve gas pods special ability in combat.

- **Genetic Warfare.** Probe teams (see **Probe Teams**, p. 133) can conduct genetic warfare against a base's population.

- **Obliteration.** Wiping out one of your own bases is considered an atrocity. Wiping out a base you just conquered calls for a much more severe penalty than wiping out a base you built yourself.

- **Nerve Stapling.** This is one of the lesser atrocities, evoking less outrage from the other factions since it is committed only against your own citizens. However, if you commit this act against a conquered base, it is treated much more seriously. You can nerve staple the entire population of a base, a process that eliminates both drones and talents, making Drone riots (see **Drone Riots**, p. 63) impossible for a length of 10 turns.

SPECIAL CASES

ALIEN ARTIFACTS

Alien artifacts have no defensive capability — except that they cannot be destroyed in combat. Instead, when an enemy unit attacks a square with an undefended alien artifact, or the artifact moves adjacent to an enemy, the artifact passes into the possession of the enemy faction. Likewise, when the last defender of a base falls, any alien artifacts within the base emerge and pass into the control of the attacking faction.

PROBE TEAM COMBAT

Probe teams cannot attack most units (outside of their probe abilities), but they can attack other probe teams. Probe team combat, like psi combat, is influenced by the Morale level of the two combatants (see **Psi Combat**, p. 102, and **Morale/Lifecycle**, p. 87).

107

CHAPTER 5

CONTROLLING SOCIETY

CONTROLLING SOCIETY

There's far more to building a successful empire than building facilities and pushing units around. *Sid Meier's Alpha Centauri* allows you to manipulate economic forces, diplomacy, espionage and political ideology to strengthen your faction's hold on Planet.

HQ MENU

The options on the HQ menu are your primary tools for both long-range planning and information about your faction's progress.

SOCIAL ENGINEERING [E]

This screen is used both for Social Engineering proper (see **Society Window**, p. 136), and for energy allocation (see **Energy Allocation**, p. 117).

110

SET RESEARCH PRIORITIES\CHANGE RESEARCH GOAL [Shift][R]

This option allows you to switch from one research project to another in midstream. This can be useful if, for example, the Gaians begin work on the Xenoempathy Dome (which you consider crucial to your long-term strategy), and you still haven't started research on Centauri Meditation, the prerequisite technology to building this project.

This functions in two ways, depending on whether the "Blind Research" rule was selected for your game. (See **Game Rules**, p. 197.) If "Blind Research" was selected, then you are prompted to select a new area in which to concentrate your research (see **Technology**, p. 119). If "Blind Research" was not selected, then you may choose a new technology to research.

If you elect to change research goals with "Blind Research" off, you are prompted to select a new goal. Note that if you switch research projects with "Blind Research" off, you lose half of the research you put in to the previous project (see **Switching Production**, p. 79). This means that it's better to switch projects early in the process, and best not to switch at all, unless you must. If "Blind Research" has been selected, then no research is lost.

DESIGN WORKSHOP [U]

This option leads to the Design Workshop. It is fully described under **Designing Units, p. 81.**

DATALINKS [F1]

Datalinks are the essential depository of information about Planet, the factions, technology, facilities and Secret Projects, and the fundamental concepts behind *Sid Meier's Alpha Centauri.*

REPORT READOUTS

The next eight options on the HQ menu are your report readouts. They contain an abundance of information about your current status in the game.

Each of the report screens has a DATALINKS button to open the Datalinks, and a CANCEL button to close the screen. Also, along the bottom of each report screen is a line of icon but-

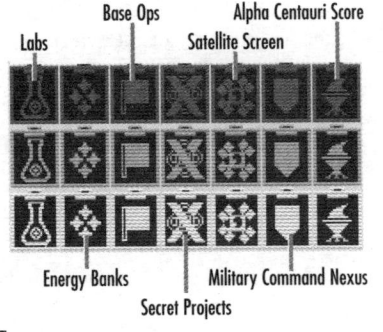

Base Ops
Alpha Centauri Score
Labs
Satellite Screen
Energy Banks
Military Command Nexus
Secret Projects

tons, each one of which takes you directly to one of the other report screens. (The button for the current screen is highlighted.)

In the center of each screen (near the game year) is a large colored icon that represents your faction. Next to it may be a series of smaller, monochrome icons. These icons represent other factions whose Report Readouts you have access to. You can gain access to another faction's report screens either by placing an infiltrator in the faction (either through probe team action – see **Probe Teams, p. 133** – by becoming Planetary Governor, or by constructing the Empath Guild Secret Project) or by forming a Pact Brotherhood with a fac-

111

tion. 🖰 on the faction's icon to switch to that faction's report screen, or on the large colored icon to see your own.

LABORATORIES STATUS F2

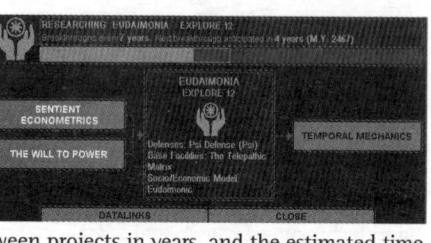

This screen displays a great deal of information about your current research project.

At the top of the screen is the name of the technology being researched, the average time between projects in years, and the estimated time to complete the current project. Below that is the technology tree (see **Technology**, p. 119), focused on the current research goal.

In the lower center of the screen, above the research screen icons, is the current year, the cost of the current project in technology points (see **Technology**, p. 119), the amount of technology points currently amassed towards that project, and the tech points your faction accrues each turn.

The lower left corner of the screen is an MFD (multi-function display). 🖰 on "Technology" for a list of technologies your faction has already acquired. 🖰 on "Bases" for a list of all your bases, each with its technology output each turn. You can 🖰 on a base to open its Base Control Screen.

The lower right corner of the screen is a series of bar graphs, each one displaying how far you've progressed along each technology track.

ENERGY BANKS F3

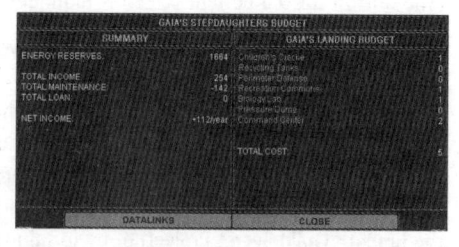

This screen offers a detailed rundown of your faction's budget.

The **Summary** window records total energy reserves, net income, gross income and maintenance expenses for the entire faction, as well as loan payment income and a breakdown of all active loans (including loan payments suspended due to vendetta; see **Diplomatic Contact**, p. 127).

The **Bases** window, in the lower left corner of the screen, displays gross income, expenses and net income (or deficit) for each base. 🖱 on a base to see its facilities, facilities maintenance and total energy.

The **Maintenance** window lists each type of base facility that your faction has currently built, showing the total number of such facilities and the total maintenance cost per turn for all facilities of that type. 🖱 on a facility to see which bases possess that facility.

BASE OPERATIONS STATUS F4

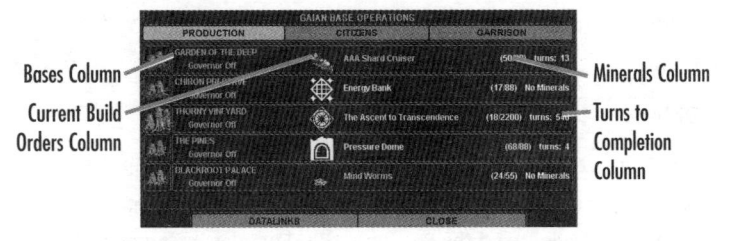

Bases Column
Current Build
Orders Column
— Minerals Column
Turns to
Completion
Column

113

This screen provides a detailed breakdown of how each of your faction's bases is currently engaged.

The large upper MFD displays the name, icon and current governor setting for each of your bases. You can 🖱 on a base's name to select that base, or double-🖱 to go directly to that base. You can also 🖱 a base's name for a list of command options, including opening the Base Control Screen, centering the Main Map on the base, changing production, hurrying the current build orders, or changing the Governor settings. You can also change the Governor settings if you 🖱 on the base icon. (See **Bases**, p. 58, for more on these options.)

If one base is selected, its location on the world map will be shown (lower right corner).

🖰 on **Production** to see each base's current build orders, how many minerals have been accrued towards those orders, total mineral cost of those orders, and estimated number of turns until completion. For more on **Build Orders**, see p. 67.

Citizens displays the population graph for each base, showing the function and attitude of each citizen. 🖰 on a worker to reassign as a specialist, and 🖰 on a specialist to reassign as a worker (see **Citizens**, p. 61).

Garrison shows each unit currently stationed in each base. 🖰 on a unit for a menu of options to activate the unit or give it orders.

- Activate

- Edit Unit (appears only when scenario editor is activated, see **Appendix 4: Advanced Customization**, p. 206)

- Sentry/Board Transport

- Hold

- Disband

For more information on these commands, see **Action Menu**, p. 92.

A smaller MFD is located in the lower left of the screen. This MFD may display the Governor Readout and the Best Bases Readout, depending on which of the two buttons you have selected.

The **Governor Readout** allows you to apply any of the normal governor options (see **Governor**, p. 69). You can change the governor options for a specific base (the base highlighted in the upper MFD), or choose SELECT ALL to simultaneously change every base in your faction. Ctrl 🖰 on each of several bases to select multiple bases.

The **Best Bases Readout** shows your top-performing base in each of several categories, including mineral, nutrient and energy production, energy reserves, lab output, Psych output, population and garrisoned units.

SECRET PROJECT DATA [F5]

Displays all Secret Projects currently either completed or under construction, with their location and the controlling faction. Projects in progress are located above completed

projects, showing every faction working on a given project at the moment. If the same faction is working on the same Secret Project at two or more bases, only the base which is furthest along towards completion is displayed. 🖰 on a base to see where it is located on the map (lower right).

ORBITAL AND SPACE STATIONS [F6]

Displays all known orbital facilities currently in orbit. You can 🖰 **Orbital Attack View** to engage in satellite warfare. If you have any orbital defense pods, you may select an enemy faction in the lower left MFD and which type of satellite of theirs you want to attack in the lower right MFD. An **ATTACK!** button will appear for you to confirm your attack.

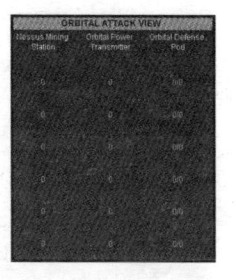

115

MILITARY COMMAND NEXUS [F7]

Displays the name, icon and basic stats for every unit prototype your faction has produced or is producing. The number of units active, in production and lost in combat is given

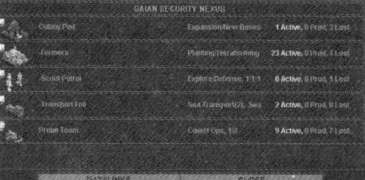

for each unit prototype. Types of units (land, naval, air and non-combat) are listed in the lower left window. 🖰 on a unit type in this window to see all units of this type.

ALPHA CENTAURI SCORE [F8]

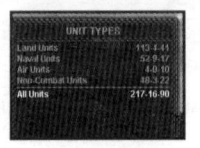

Displays your current score. (See **Scoring**, p. 145.)

COMMUNICATIONS AND PROTOCOL [F12]

Displays the Commlink menu (see **Commlink**, p. 23), which allows you to contact other factions.

HALL OF FAME

This is a list of the best scoring games, by faction.

Corner Global Energy Market

This option only appears after you've discovered Sentient Econometrics. By selecting this option, you may try to control Planet by cornering the global energy market (See **Winning the Game**, p. 143).

Review Scenario Objectives

This option only appears if you are playing a scenario, and contains information about your objectives and score status.

ECONOMICS

Cash flow has been a headache of civilized society since the Sumerians decided that building a city might be a neat idea. This will not change in the future. The productivity of your faction depends largely on the output of the individual bases (see **Base Management: The Essentials**, p. 58), but there are also fundamental policy decisions that can affect how efficiently your faction exploits the resources it gathers.

ENERGY ALLOCATION

Total Economy Collected Each Turn

Number of Turns between Research Breakthroughs

"Lock" Icon

SOCIAL ENGINEERING

Energy Income: 68
Breakthroughs: 3 turns

PSYCH 40%   LABS 30%

Each of your bases requires a certain amount of energy to maintain. It is up to you, however, to decide how to best allocate your energy surplus. There are three priorities among which you must divide your energy resources: Labs, Psych and Economy.

Adjusting Energy Allocation. You allocate your energy using the three sliding bars on the bottom of the Social Engineering Screen (see **HQ Menu**, p. 110). You can increase or decrease any of the bars in increments of 10% (of your total energy budget) if you 🖰 on the arrow icons: left to decrease, right to increase. When you get one of the values to where you want it, you can 🖰 on the lock icon to lock it down, and thereafter all exchanges are between the other two values. (Otherwise the game decides how to add or subtract energy when you alter the levels.)

At the start of the game your energy allocation is set to 50% Labs, 50% Economy and 0% Psych.

- **Labs.** Lab investments go directly to research. The more you invest, the faster you discover new technologies, facilities and Secret Projects.

- **Psych.** This investment is spent on recreation, culture and basic luxuries. The more you invest in Psych, the more workers become talents, offsetting the malcontent drones in your bases (see **Citizens**, p. 61).

- **Economy.** Energy reserved for Economy goes to support your existing base facilities, with any excess stored in your energy reserve. The more you invest in Economy, the more wealth you have available for emergencies.

117

Making radical adjustments in your allocation levels creates inefficiency. This loss to inefficiency is displayed on the Social Engineering Screen (a high Efficiency rating — see **Social Factors,** p. 141 — can diminish such losses). In general, the greater the difference between your Labs and Economy settings, the more inefficiency occurs.

INEFFICIENCY

As your faction expands to new bases, the bureaucracy required to administer it grows more unwieldy. The net result of this inevitable process is inefficiency — a certain amount of resources that a base collects are never available for actual use. The efficiency of any given base is directly related to both its size and its distance from your faction HQ. Larger, more remote bases are most prone to inefficiency.

The primary way to combat inefficiency is through Social Engineering (see **Society Window,** p. 136), but inefficiency can also be curtailed via certain facilities, such as the Children's Creche. Relocating your headquarters to a central location can also help control inefficiency.

You create a different kind of inefficiency when you adjust your energy allocations in extreme ways (see **Energy Allocation,** p. 117). This inefficiency reflects the principle of diminishing returns—past a certain point, the more effort you put towards a particular priority, the less the effect of the increased effort.

TECHNOLOGY

The success of your faction on Planet is judged, to a great extent, on your ability to acquire new technology.

Scientific breakthroughs are a large part of technology advances, but they're not the whole story. For example, any primitive tribesman of old Earth could hollow out a tree and make a canoe, but your faction can't build sea-going units until it acquires Doctrine: Flexibility. This isn't because water works differently on Planet, it's because it takes a great deal of work, planning and inspiration to set up a self-sustaining shipbuilding industry of the sort required to produce high-tech, ocean-going vessels on command.

Many of these technologies combine a new scientific discovery with a new way of looking at the world. The result is usually quite useful.

RESEARCH

Your faction can research only one technology at a time. When you acquire a new tech, you begin research on your next discovery. Most technologies can only be researched after certain other technologies—its "prerequisites"—have already been discovered, so as you advance technologically, your options grow and change. Your research efforts can be augmented by allocating more energy to Labs, building base laboratory facilities, and creating scientifically oriented specialists in your bases (see **Appendix 2: Technology Tree**, p. 185, for a list of all technologies).

119

BLIND RESEARCH

Normally (unless you disable the option during game setup) your research is "blind." You do not select a specific research goal. Instead, you are asked to choose a research priority, and your goal is randomly selected according to that preference. You can select multiple priorities, which increases the number of technologies available under your preferences.

If you disable blind research, you select specific technologies to work towards.

However, the list of available technologies at any given time is random, and does not necessarily include every technology for which you have completed the prerequisites.

THE TECH TREE

Technology advances are like building a house—you have to start at the bottom and work up. Technologies are not discovered in a vacuum; each new discovery depends on everything that's gone before it. In *Sid Meier's Alpha Centauri*, the underlying structure that determines the order of breakthroughs is called the Tech Tree. When you first land on Planet there are a few initial technologies towards which you may begin to direct your research. From this foundation you begin to build the technological superstructure of human civilization on Planet.

The entire tech tree is displayed on the poster included with this game. You can also view the tech tree in the game itself, using the Datalinks or the F2 hotkey. In the Datalinks, techs with white lettering are those you've already discovered, techs with dark lettering remain to be discovered.

Prerequisites. With the exception of the first seven technologies, each new technology requires that at least one and usually two other technologies be acquired before it can even be researched. These precursor technologies are the prerequisites of the new technology (which in turn is a prerequisite for one or more technologies to come). Knowing the prerequisites for an important technology is an essential part of formulating an effective research strategy. For example, if you want to be the first faction to learn Secrets of the Human Brain (and obtain the bonus technology that distinction brings you), you must know that you have to discover Social Psych and Biogenetics first.

Prerequisites for a given technology can be found in the Datalinks of the game, and are shown on the Tech Tree poster.

Tracks and Levels. The technology tree is divided into four technology tracks. These divisions have no direct game effect, but they do make it easier to keep track of your progress up the tech tree. The four tracks are:

- **Explore.** Discoveries that make it easier to unravel the secrets of Planet.

- **Discover.** Theoretical breakthroughs in the realm of "pure science."

- **Build.** New technologies that enhance the infrastructure of your faction and its bases.

- **Conquer.** Military advances.

The levels simply record how far along the track a given technology lies. For example, Monopole Magnets, the discovery that makes the mag tube enhancement possible, is Build 6, expressed as B6. When trading techs with other factions, you can compare these numbers, to get an idea of which faction is getting the better deal.

ACQUIRING TECHNOLOGY

Your scientists in their research labs drive your technology acquisition. But there are several other ways to pick up tech, and it's in your best interest to exploit as many of them as possible.

Research. As long as you have any energy allocated to Labs, your faction conducts research.

Unity **Pods.** Some of the pods left by the *Unity* contain downloads from the Datalinks of old Earth which, when combined with your own discoveries, can provide the key to unlock a new technology instantaneously.

Alien Artifacts. These esoteric devices can be taken to a base and linked with that base's network node (if it has one). Such a linkage inevitably provides an instant tech advance. Normally, the network node for any given base can only be linked to a single artifact (the Universal Translator Secret Project is the only exception to this rule—you may link any number of artifacts to it).

Diplomacy. One of the most common forms of diplomacy, particularly early in the game, is for the leader of another faction to offer to trade a technology you need for a technology he or she needs. Sometimes he or she also offers to trade technology for a copy of a world map, or even for energy credits. Sometimes, the other faction just demands that you fork a tech over unilaterally. You can initiate similar requests to the other leaders (see **Diplomatic Contact**, p. 127).

Probe Teams. Probe teams can steal technology from other factions (see **Probe Teams** p. 133).

Secrets Technologies. The three "secrets" technologies (Secrets of the Human Brain, Secrets of Alpha Centauri, Secrets of Creation) each provide an extra instant tech advance to the *first* faction to discover them.

Secret Projects. The Universal Translator gives the faction that builds it two instant tech advances immediately after it's built. The Planetary Datalinks give you instant access to any technology that is already known to any three other factions. The Network Backbone and Supercollider can greatly enhance your tech output.

Conquest. In some games (depending on what rules options you selected; see **Game Rules**, p. 195) conquering an enemy base allows you to select any one of that faction's technologies that you do not already possess.

THE USES OF TECHNOLOGY

The biggest reason to research new technology is that it lets you build new things—units, facilities and Secret Projects. That's not all it does, however.

Technology can also:

Increase your production. Certain discoveries lift caps on the maximum amount of a given resource you can take from a given square. Other discoveries increase your ability to take resources from fungus squares. See **Fungus Production**, p. 43.

Expand your infrastructure. Some later discoveries can make certain key base facilities part of your infrastructure—they are added to every new base that's built, at the time of establishment (bases that were built before the discovery have to build the facility normally). See **Facilities**, p. 64.

Grant access to specialists, enhancements and social options. New technologies can give you access to new specialists (making current technologies obsolete), new terraforming enhancements, and new social options (see **Society Window**, p. 136).

DIPLOMACY

The least predictable part of your own faction's survival on Planet is dealing with the other six factions. Each of the other faction leaders is a distinct personality, with his or her own goals, motivations and temperament. You have to know when to get tough and when to ease off, when giving a little yields long-term rewards and when it just makes you seem weak.

FACTIONS

Each faction behaves in a manner consistent with its individual nature. The philosophies of the factions mentioned below are explained beginning on p. 11.

Distinguishing data for the factions is given in several categories:

- **Faction Characteristics** are adjustments to social factors that are intrinsic to that faction.

- **Aggression** indicates how eager the faction is for a fight. There are three levels: Aggressive, Erratic, Pacifist.

123

- **Priorities** represent what's most important to the faction. There are four possible priorities:

    Explore (The faction seeks to occupy as much territory as possible)

    Discover (The faction seeks to discover new technologies)

    Build (The faction seeks to build up its bases as much as possible)

    Conquer (The faction seeks to maximize military strength)

- **Starting Tech** is any technologies that the faction automatically possesses at the start of the game.

- **Agendas** are Social Engineering choices that the faction *always* makes, when available.

- **Aversions** are Social Engineering choices that the faction *never* makes.

BELIEVERS
Faction Characteristics

+25% Bonus when attacking enemies, from the strength of convictions.

+1 Probe (devout believers difficult to brainwash)

-2 Research (suspicious of secular science)

-1 Planet (believe Planet is their promised land)

Accumulates no research points until MY 2110.

May not use Knowledge value in Social Engineering.

Aggression	Aggressive
Priorities	Explore, Conquer
Starting Tech	Social Psych
Agenda	Fundamentalist (Politics)
Aversion	Knowledge (Values)

GAIANS
Faction Characteristics

+1 Planet (environmental safeguards; can capture mind worms)

+2 Efficiency (experience with life systems & recycling)

-1 Morale (pacifist tendencies)

-1 Police (freedom-loving)

+1 Nutrients in fungus squares

May not use Free Market economics.

Aggression	Pacifist
Priorities	Explore
Starting Tech	Centauri Ecology
Agenda	Green (Economics)
Aversion	Free Market (Economics)

HIVE

Faction Characteristics

+1 Growth (rapid population growth)

+1 Industry (brutal serfdom)

-2 Economy (little political freedom)

Underground bunkers (free Perimeter Defense at each base)

May not use Democratic politics.

Aggression	Aggressive
Priorities	Conquer, Build
Starting Tech	Doctrine: Loyalty
Agenda	Police State (Politics)
Aversion	Democracy (Politics)

MORGAN INDUSTRIES

Faction Characteristics

125

+1 Economy (industrial conglomerate)

-1 Support (followers have expensive tastes)

Commerce (bonus increases value of treaties, pacts, loans)

Begins with 100 extra energy credits.

Need Hab Complex for bases to exceed size 4 (creature comforts at a premium).

May not use Planned Economics.

Aggression	Pacifist
Priorities	Build
Starting Tech	Industrial Economics
Agenda	Free Market (Economics)
Aversion	Planned (Economics)

PEACEKEEPERS

Faction Characteristics

-1 Efficiency (U.N.-style bureaucracy)

Extra talent for every four citizens (attracts intellectual elite)

May exceed Hab Complex population requirements by 2.

Receives double votes in elections for Planetary Governor and Supreme Leader.

May not use Police State Politics.

Aggression	Erratic
Priorities	Explore, Discover
Starting Tech	Biogenetics
Agenda	Democracy (Politics)
Aversion	Police State (Politics)

SPARTANS

Faction Characteristics

+2 Morale (well armed survivalist movement)

+1 Police (highly disciplined followers)

-1 Industry (extravagant weapons are costly)

Prototype units do not cost extra minerals.

May not use Wealth value in Social Engineering.

Aggression	Erratic
Priorities	Discover, Conquer
Starting Tech	Doctrine: Mobility
Agenda	Power (Values)
Aversion	Wealth (Values)

UNIVERSITY
Faction Characteristics

+2 Research (brilliant research)

-2 Probe (academic networks vulnerable to infiltration)

Free network node at every base

One bonus tech at beginning of game

Extra drone for every four citizens (lack of ethics)

May not use Fundamentalist Politics.

Aggression	Erratic
Priorities	Discover
Starting Tech	Information Networks, +1 bonus tech
Agenda	Knowledge (Values)
Aversion	Fundamentalist (Politics)

DIPLOMATIC CONTACT

Before you can contact any of the other faction leaders, you must first have their commlink frequencies. This is usually gained by coming into direct contact with one of that faction's units, but can also be gained from a third faction, or sometimes even found in a *Unity* pod. The Empath Guild Secret Project also grants you the comm frequency of every faction leader.

When one of your units or bases comes into contact with the unit or base of another faction for the first time, you usually open communications with the faction's leader. If you talk to another leader once, you exchange comm frequencies. Once frequencies are exchanged, the other leader might contact you, or you can contact him or her using your Commlink menu (see **Commlink,** p. 23). When another leader calls, you don't have to answer, and likewise he/she might sometimes ignore your communications (particularly in hostile situations). Once communications are underway, there are many options.

Sometimes communications are terse—a curt demand that a unit be removed from faction territory, or a to-the-point death threat—but many are quite involved conversations. At any point during communication you can consult the Datalinks for information about the faction, technology they may be requesting, or military units.

When you are in communication with another faction leader, he or she might start off by offering you an alliance against a common enemy, or offering to improve your diplomatic relations status (see **Diplomatic Relations**, facing page). They'll often offer to trade technology or world maps, and they'll frequently demand tribute of tech or energy (sometimes expressed as a "fine" for some unspecified infraction of their faction legalities). They'll often tell you about their latest military innovation, to let you know they're ready for trouble. They might even offer to end a vendetta between your factions. Once these preliminaries are over, it's your turn. Your options are:

OFFER A PROPOSAL

Proposals that may be offered include:

- A **gift**, or "token of your esteem," consisting of technology (one or all of your available technologies), energy credits, or even one of your bases. This makes a leader more friendly towards you, and if the gift is truly significant, she might forgive your past transgressions.

- **Upgrading diplomatic relations** (truce to treaty, or treaty to pact brotherhood). If your first proposal is accepted, you can try to upgrade again immediately.

- A **request for technology**, either as extortion or in trade.

- A **request for energy credits**, as extortion, in trade, or as a loan.

- A **joint attack** against a common enemy.

EXCHANGE BATTLE PLANS

You and the other faction leader discuss your immediate plans for battle, in order to coordinate your efforts. The other leader presents you with a list of targets, and you may select the target that you wish the other leader to attack.

CALL OFF VENDETTA

You request the other faction leader call off his or her vendetta against a third faction.

REQUEST VOTE

You request that the other faction leader support you in an upcoming council session. Often such support comes at a steep price.

TERRITORY VIOLATION

You demand that the other leader immediately remove all his or her units from your territory.

DIPLOMATIC RELATIONS

Your relations with any other faction at any given moment depend on a number of factors, including your social choices, your proximity to their territory, your military power, and of course your reputation and behavior during prior diplomatic communications. When a faction leader is in communication, you are given a one-word summary of that faction's attitude towards you and of their reported military preparedness.

Mood	*Might*
(*best to worst*)	(*strongest to weakest*)
Magnanimous (Submissive*)	Unsurpassed
Solicitous	Potent
Cooperative	Formidable
Noncommittal	Sufficient
Ambivalent	Wanting
Obstinate	Anemic
Quarrelsome	Feeble
Belligerent	
Seething	

*This is a special case of Magnanimous, encountered when the faction is hopelessly overmatched.

Mood is based on several factors, including how honest you've been with that faction in the past, whether you've ever committed an atrocity against the faction, and how powerful you are in relation to that faction—faction leaders get touchy and defensive when someone else is far stronger than they are. Small factions often ally together to oppose very strong factions, even if the stronger faction has behaved honorably.

Once you are in communication with a faction, your relationship settles into one of four categories:

VENDETTA

A state of war exists. Each faction is under no obligation whatsoever to respect the other's territory, and you can attack one another's units and bases with impunity. Any loan payments are suspended.

TRUCE

A state of "watchful peace." While the truce is in effect, the other faction may not honorably attack your units, but may move his units into your territory (you may attempt to threaten or cajole him into withdrawing). Loan payments are made on schedule.

TREATY

A state of peace and cooperation. Both factions are expected to keep military units out of the other's territory (or at least remove them promptly when asked). The bases of two factions with a treaty conduct commerce with one another (see Commerce, facing page).

PACT OF BROTHERHOOD

A full diplomatic alliance. Both sides share their world maps, can access the other's report readouts (see HQ Menu, p. 110), and may move freely through one another's territory (zones of control do not apply between pact brothers).

Units from one faction may even visit the other's bases for repairs and leave units in the same square. Income from commerce is increased. If one pact brother declares vendetta against a third faction, the pact partner is expected to do the same.

COMMERCE

If you have a treaty or pact with another faction, the two factions' bases automatically conduct trade with one another. The amount of commerce income depends on your respective social choices and the size of the bases involved. Pact Brotherhood results in more profitable commerce than a simple treaty—commerce rates are doubled.

The largest bases in the two factions trade with one another, as do the two next largest, and so on until one side or the other runs out of bases.

TERRITORY

Any squares which are nearer to one of your bases than to any other faction's base are considered your territory. Territory cannot extend more than seven squares out from a land base, or three squares out from sea bases, and must be on the same continent (or sea) as the base claiming it. Building a base close to another faction's territory may cause boundaries to be re-drawn. It is entirely possible for bases from rival factions to be so close that the territorial boundary runs through both bases' production radii.

INTEGRITY

As you interact with the other factions, you inevitably gain a reputation. This is based less on your belligerence than upon your honesty. You can attack literally everyone you see, but if you don't break any treaties or commit any atrocities while doing so your honor remains unbesmirched.

The levels of integrity are:

Noble	Scrupulous	Ruthless
Faithful	Dependable	Treacherous

You can wreck your good name by breaking treaties and committing atrocities. If your integrity is towards the "treacherous" end of the scale, other factions are less likely to make deals with you, and more likely to break any treaties that do exist.

PLANETARY COUNCIL

The final tool of diplomacy on Planet is the Planetary Council. You can convene this body at any time, once you have the comm frequencies of all the factions.

No leader can call the council more than once every 20 years (except the planetary governor, who can call the council every ten years), and at each meeting it can consider only one proposal. (Electing a leader does not count against this limit, however.) No single proposal can be considered more than once every 20 years.

The first order of business for the council is probably electing a Planetary Governor. This post mostly consists of chairing council meetings, but the Governor does gain an increase to trade and better intelligence against the other factions. The most direct power of the Planetary Governor is the power of veto over any council actions—the governor's veto can only be overridden if all of the other leaders unite against it. In the vote for Planetary Governor, it is entirely acceptable to cast your vote for yourself. When an election is called, you see whom each faction is publicly supporting for the election, but this may not be who they actually vote for.

In votes for Planetary Governor (and later, in votes for Supreme Leader), each faction is given a variable number of votes in council depending on its population. The voice of a larger, richer faction counts for far more than the voice of the small and weak. Only the leaders with the two largest vote totals are eligible to stand for Planetary Governor or Supreme Leader.

Other council actions are decided by simple majority vote (subject to veto by the Planetary Governor). Matters that may be brought before the council include:

- **Salvage *Unity* Fusion Core.** The rare elements from the *Unity*'s core provide 500 energy credits to each faction.

- **Global Trade Pact.** Increases income from inter-faction commerce.

- **Launch Solar Shade.** Causes temperatures to drop world wide, making sea levels go down.

- **Melt Polar Caps.** Causes global warming, making sea levels go up.

- **Repeal UN Charter.** All atrocity prohibitions are removed.

- **Reinstate UN Charter.** If the council chooses to repeal the charter, it can later vote to reinstate it.

Not all of these options are necessarily available at any given council meeting. Many of the more radical terraforming operations have prerequisite technologies that must be discovered before they can be proposed.

In your regular communications with other council members you may request that they vote your way in council. You can even offer them "special considerations" (bribes) in exchange for their votes.

PROBE TEAMS

Somewhere between war and diplomacy is the realm of the spy. Probe Teams combine espionage and electronic warfare, plus a fair dose of terrorism in their capabilities. An effectively coordinated program of Probe Team operations can, all by itself, give your faction a decisive advantage in the ongoing contest for supremacy.

Probe teams cannot attack other units directly, but they can battle one another to the death. Probe Team combat is based on the morale of the combatants. Probe Teams can attack other teams even in squares containing other units. Since Probe Teams have no "official" existence, destroying another faction's Probe Teams does not violate a treaty or pact.

PROBE TEAM ACTIONS

Probe Teams are covert ops agents. They infiltrate the bases and territory of other factions and conduct espionage and sabotage.

Some Probe Team actions require an investment of energy. How much depends on the severity of the action and the enemy's strength. Most major Probe Team actions are legitimate grounds for Vendetta and, in the event you are caught, may cause your reputation among the other factions to suffer (See Integrity, p. 131.)

When you initiate any Probe Team action, you are shown your chance of success, expressed as a pair of percentages (the higher your Probe Team's morale, the better the odds). The first percentage shown is the team's chance of completing the operation, the second is its chance of escaping alive. When a Probe Team enters a base or any square containing an enemy unit, it may attempt the following actions:

INFILTRATE DATALINKS

The probe team hacks into the faction's Datalinks. This greatly increases your intelligence data about that faction, including access to their report readouts, and even individual base readouts.

STEAL TECHNOLOGY

Just what it says. You grab the other faction's research technology. You may try for a specific technology, or grab one at random. Attempts to steal specific technology are much more difficult.

SABOTAGE BASE

You can either destroy an existing facility, wreck Planet Buster silos, or wipe out all minerals accrued towards that base's current build orders. You may target a specific facility, or destroy something at random. Attempts to sabotage a specific facility are much more difficult. You cannot sabotage faction HQ or Secret Projects. Perimeter Defenses and Tachyon Fields are *extremely* hard to target.

MIND CONTROL

Mind control is an attempt to subvert a base or unit of a rival faction and bring it under your control.

The attractive aspect to unit mind control is that it's one of the few probe activities that don't need to be carried out from inside an enemy base—your Probe Team can lurk in the wilderness or near your territorial borders and swoop down to grab any unit that gets too close. Only single units may be targeted by Probe Teams. Multiple units in a square are invulnerable to mind control.

The *Total Thought Control* option is a variant of mind control that takes control of a base or unit, without causing any damage to your reputation with the other factions. It costs the same as normal mind control, but has a lower chance of success.

The cost of a mind control operation against a base depends on a number of factors, including the base's size, the enemy's energy reserves, facilities and special operations in a base, and whether or not drone riots are occurring.

A Probe Team cannot take control of a base containing a faction's headquarters.

135

INCREASE DRONE ACTIVITY

This operation changes one Worker or Talent in the enemy base into a Drone. This is a useful preliminary operation to a mind control attempt, since a base embroiled in drone riots is significantly easier and less expensive to mind control.

DRAIN ENERGY RESERVES

This ambitious operation attempts to divert a portion of the faction's energy reserves to your accounts. The more reserves the faction has, the more you stand to gain.

GENETIC WARFARE

This is considered a severe atrocity. A successful genetic warfare operation decreases the population of the base by a full 50%, instantaneously. Units inside the base also lose strength to the virus.

DEFENDING VS. PROBE TEAMS

Other than physically hunting them down and destroying them, your best defense against enemy Probe Teams is to boost your Probe rating through Social Engineering (see **Society Window**, below). Investing energy towards Psych also tends to deter Probe activities (see **Energy Allocation**, p. 117).

An excellent deterrent to enemy Probe Team activity is simply to station one of your own Probe Teams in strategically important bases. An enemy Probe Team must engage and destroy your team before it can undertake any further operations.

The Hunter-Seeker Algorithm Secret Project makes your entire faction immune to probe activity.

SOCIAL ENGINEERING

Your faction has a purpose, a reason for existing, and that purpose is more than just dominating all the other factions. Social engineering is the way you put your social and political philosophy into action. Every Social Engineering choice you make carries both benefits and liabilities for your faction. It is your job to see that the benefits support your long-term strategy, and the liabilities do not significantly detract from it.

Social engineering represents the fundamental defining characteristics of your faction's society. The choices you make in regard to these fundamentals literally affect every aspect of your faction. Use E or select Social Engineering from your HQ menu to access the Social Engineering Readout.

SOCIETY WINDOW

The Society Window is the upper portion of your Social Engineering Readout (the bottom portion, dealing with Energy Allocation, is described under Energy Allocation, p. 117). This is where you actually pick the underpinnings of your society. It consists of four lines, each representing a fundamental decision, and four choices for each line. You may make one choice from each line.

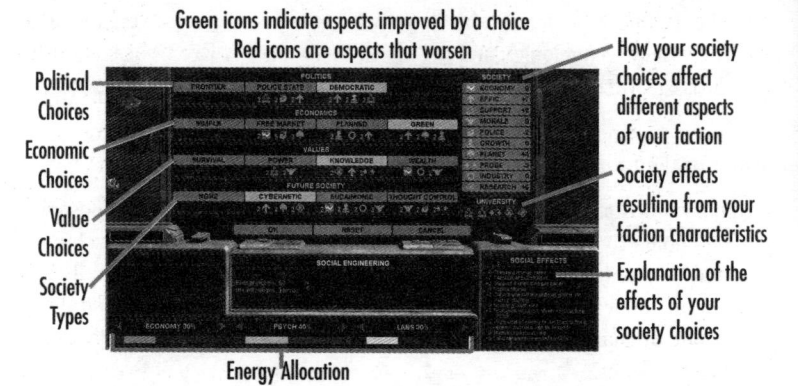

Green icons indicate aspects improved by a choice
Red icons are aspects that worsen

Political Choices

Economic Choices

Value Choices

Society Types

How your society choices affect different aspects of your faction

Society effects resulting from your faction characteristics

Explanation of the effects of your society choices

Energy Allocation

These choices determine your society's base rating in each of the social factor categories (see below). At the start of the game only the default values (Frontier, Simple, Survival, None) are available, and you have no choices to make. As your technology progresses, your options expand and you must choose how to continue.

Each choice's effects on your social factors are displayed in the form of icons. Green icons are positive modifiers, red icons are negative modifiers.

There are several sub-windows on the Society Window. The one in the upper right displays the meaning of each category icon, and your current rating in each category. Also, if you 🖱 on any one category, your social choices arrange themselves so that that category is optimized—"maxed out." If you do this, make sure you look carefully at the other ratings, to make sure you haven't created a dangerous deficit in some other category.

The window in the lower left simply provides a detailed breakdown of each choice, as you pass your cursor over that category. *This window may be used by players who cannot read the color coding in the main window.*

The window on the right is a detailed breakdown of the effects of your current choices in every category.

In the middle is a display showing your current energy reserves, the time between new technologies, and the upheaval cost, if any (see **Upheaval Costs**, below), to switch to the new choices you have tentatively selected.

You can always hit RESET to restore your choices to the way they were at the start of the turn.

Upheaval Costs. When you try to make a radical shift in political philosophy, there's going to be some social upheaval. To get your faction "over the hump" to the new order, you may be required to pay some energy credits. This is called an "upheaval cost." You can eliminate or mitigate it by slowing down your rate of change, making the move to the final new order gradually over a number of turns.

POLITICS

How your faction reaches policy decisions.

- **Frontier.** The default. Frontier politics represent the informal governing arrangements made in early colonies, before populations reach levels requiring more advanced forms of government. **No positives or negatives.**

- **Police State.** Police states use oppression to keep their citizens in line, and allow their leaders great power over military decisions. However, oppression of this sort also decreases economic efficiency. **+2 Support, +2 Police, -2 Efficiency**

- **Democratic.** Democracies allow citizens to participate in government, and forego oppression and the stability it confers in favor of growth and efficiency. However, citizens remain suspicious of large military deployments, and civilian oversight creates large military bureaucracies, so military support costs increase. **+2 Efficiency, +2 Growth, -2 Support**

- **Fundamentalist.** Fundamentalist politics unite a society behind a strong, dogmatic religion. Evangelizing the populace can create loyal, even fanatical military forces, and tends to immunize citizens against (other forms of) brainwashing. However, technological research tends to suffer under the continual assaults on intellectual integrity associated with such regimes. **+2 Probe, +1 Morale, -2 Research**

ECONOMICS

How your faction administers its resources.

- **Simple.** The default. Simple economics describes the informal, ad hoc economy that develops in the early years after planetfall, before more organized economic systems can be put in place. **No positives or negatives.**

- **Free Market.** Free market economics turns market forces loose in your society. Unfettered market economics can produce great wealth quickly, but in the context of Planet's fragile emerging economies can also lead to extremes of pollution and ecological damage. Also, citizens rendered suddenly poor by the actions of unscrupulous moguls may revolt against their energy-fattened masters. **+2 Economy, -3 Planet, -5 Police**

- **Planned.** A semi-market economy kept in check by fierce governmental regulation, planned economics promotes stable industrial and population growth, but sacrifices efficiency. **+2 Growth, +1 Industry, -2 Efficiency**

- **Green.** Green economics strive to integrate human progress with the needs of the biosphere. Green economies use resources efficiently and tend to avoid the excesses of industrial development which could provoke Planet's native life, but population growth necessarily suffers due to lack of space. **+2 Efficiency, +2 Planet, -2 Growth**

139

VALUES

The goals your society thinks are most important.

- **Survival.** Simple survival is, of course, the all-encompassing first priority of early human space colonies. **No positives or negatives.**

- **Power.** Leaders seeking power build strong, well paid military forces to enforce their will. However, economic and industrial infrastructure may suffer from bloated "defense" budgets. **+2 Support, +2 Morale, -2 Industry**

- **Knowledge.** Leaders seeking knowledge and intellectual enlightenment pour resources into research and education. They also tend to promote the free exchange of information, which increases efficiency but also carries greater security risks. **+2 Research, +1 Efficiency, -2 Probe**

- **Wealth.** Leaders seeking wealth concentrate on building economic and industrial infrastructure rapidly. They achieve rapid growth and development, with possible side effects being decadence and moral decay. **+1 Economy, +1 Industry, -2 Morale**

FUTURE SOCIETY

Powerful doctrines of social development arising from advanced theories of Social Engineering.

- **None.** The default. Your society has not yet evolved to a far future society. **No positives or negatives.**

- **Cybernetic.** In the far future, citizens may turn many of the tasks of governing society over to artificially intelligent computers, increasing efficiency and freeing humans for more creative tasks. But will workers displaced by computers sink into despair, poverty, and possible unrest? **+2 Efficiency, +2 Planet, +2 Research, -3 Police**

- **Eudaimonic.** Perhaps the most pleasant to contemplate living in, this far future society takes its name from an ancient Greek word for fulfillment and happiness. Eudaimonic society encourages each citizen to achieve happiness through striving to fulfill completely his or her potential. Population, economy and industry all experience healthy growth. Violence fades as society grows more tolerant and just, and even when this society's hand is forced it often shoots to subdue rather than to destroy. **+2 Economy, +2 Growth, +2 Industry, -2 Morale**

- **Thought Control.** The ultimate in "Big Brother" methods, thought control effuses subtle neurochemical triggers into the atmosphere to render its population obedient, loyal and resistant to outside ideas. However, significant resources are required to maintain this level of control. **+2 Morale, +2 Police, +2 Probe, -3 Support**

SOCIAL FACTORS

Your faction possesses a numerical ranking (negative, positive or zero) in each of the following categories. Positive ratings represent assets of your society, negative ratings are liabilities. The specific results of each ranking in each factor are found in the table in **Appendix 2: Social Factors**, p. 158.

Although they're most directly determined by your social choices (see **Society Window**, p. 136), these ratings are also directly affected by your original faction philosophy, and several Secret Projects. Several base facilities can change the ratings for that base only. Children's Creche, for example, increases the Growth rating for each base that builds one.

ECONOMY

Increases or decreases energy production by squares and by base; also increases or decreases commerce income (see **Commerce**, p. 131).

EFFICIENCY

Increases or decreases loss due to inefficiency or modification of energy allocation (see **Energy Allocation**, p. 117).

SUPPORT

Increases or decreases the cost to support units outside of your base. High ratings can give you a number of units that can be supported "for free" (see **Home Base, Support and Pacifism**, p. 89).

MORALE

Increases or decreases the morale of your units. Negative values can actually decrease the combat readiness of units (see **Morale/Lifecycle**, p. 87).

POLICE

Determines the number of units that can act as police (see **Drone Riots**, p. 63) in your bases. Factions with a Police rating of ñ3 or less are considered Pacifist, and produce more drones when units are stationed outside the base (see **Home Base, Support and Pacifism**, p. 89).

GROWTH

Speeds or slows your population growth rate (see **Nutrient Tanks**, p. 68).

PLANET

Negative scores increase ecological damage. Positive scores decrease damage, enhance your ability to move through fungus, and give you the power to tame indigenous life-forms (see **Fauna**, p. 40). Your Planet rating also affects your units' skill at Psi combat (see **Psi Combat**, p. 102).

PROBE

Can increase probe team morale. Increases or decreases your faction's susceptibility to probe actions (see **Probe Teams**, p. 133).

INDUSTRY

Increases or decreases the mineral costs of base projects (see **Build Orders**, p. 67).

RESEARCH

Speeds or slows your acquisition of new technology (see **Technology**, p. 119).

RESIGNING

You may retire as faction leader at any time by selecting "Resign" from the Game menu. This ends the game and computes your *Sid Meier's Alpha Centauri* score.

You must also resign if you reach the mandatory retirement year for your game or scenario. In standard games, the mandatory retirement year is M.Y. 2500 for Citizen, Specialist and Talent difficulty levels, and M.Y. 2400 for Librarian, Thinker and Transcend levels.

You will be warned 20 years before you reach mandatory retirement.

WINNING THE GAME

There are four ways to win *Sid Meier's Alpha Centauri*—conquest, diplomatic, economic or transcendence—depending on how you set your options in the setup screens.

If you are playing a scenario, it may have specific and unique victory conditions different from those listed.

CONQUEST

You may win the game by conquest if you eliminate all remaining factions. Factions that surrender and "swear a pact to serve you" count as eliminated for this purpose. If Cooperative Victory is enabled, you need not eliminate any faction with whom you have signed a Pact of Brotherhood, though no more than three non-surrendered factions may 'win together' in this manner.

DIPLOMATIC

You may win the game diplomatically by convincing enough faction leaders to unite behind you as Supreme Leader of Planet. A 3/4 vote of the Planetary Council is required to secure such election. Only the leader of one of the two factions with the highest vote totals may stand for election as Supreme Leader.

When a Supreme Leader is elected, a faction leader may choose to defy the will of the Council and refuse to submit. In this case, the Supreme Leader must, with the help of loyal factions, conquer all defiant factions to achieve a Conquest victory. Because of the military power usually required to secure election as Supreme Leader, defying the will of the Council is generally fairly suicidal. Other factions will therefore usually take this course only if you have committed atrocities against them or have grossly and repeatedly betrayed them.

You must have the Mind\Machine Interface technology before you can try for a Diplomatic Victory.

ECONOMIC

You may win an Economic Victory by cornering the Global Energy Market. You must have discovered Planetary Economics in order to pursue such a plan.

Cornering the Global Energy Market requires a sum of energy credits roughly equal to the cost to "mind control" every remaining base on Planet. When you are ready to make such an attempt, select Corner Global Energy Market from the HQ menu.

When a faction attempts to corner the Global Energy Market, all other factions are given an allotted period of time in which they can capture or destroy the cornering faction's headquarters and thereby foil the plan.

TRANSCENDENCE

The highest form of victory is the Ascent to Transcendence, the next step in the evolution of humanity. In order to ascend, you must complete an extraordinary Secret Project—the Ascent to Transcendence—which can be started only after at least one faction has completed the Voice of Planet Secret Project.

SCORING

Whether you resign or win outright, each game is given a numerical score. You can check your current score at any time with F8, or the Alpha Centauri Score option on the **HQ Menu** (see, p. 110).

Your Alpha Centauri Score is computed as follows:

- 1 point for each citizen of each base.

- If you have won a Diplomatic or Economic victory, score 1 point for each citizen of a Pact Brother's base.

- 1/2 point for each citizen of any other faction's base.

- 1/2 point for each citizen of a surrendered base.

- 1 point for each unit of commerce your bases are receiving.

- 1 point for each technology discovered.

- 10 points for each tech advance after Transcendent Thought.

- 25 points for each Secret Project.

- A Victory bonus if you have won the game (see **Winning the Game**, p. 143):

For winning by *Conquest*, you are awarded 1000 points minus 2 for every game turn elapsed. If Cooperative Victory is enabled, all Pact Brothers and Sisters participate in the win, and points are split between all winning factions based on relative population. A maximum of three Pact Brothers and Sisters may join in a win by conquest, not including those factions that have surrendered along the way.

If you win a *Diplomatic Victory*, you are awarded 1200 points minus 2 for every game turn elapsed. If Cooperative Victory is enabled and your Pact Brother or Sister is elected Supreme Leader, you are awarded half this total.

For *Economic Victory*, you are awarded 1200 points minus 2 for every game turn elapsed. If Cooperative Victory is enabled, Pact Brothers and Sisters of the winning faction receive half the bonus points.

Players who *Ascend to Transcendence* are awarded 1600 points minus 2 for every game turn elapsed. If Cooperative Victory is enabled, all Pact Brothers and Sisters participate in the win, and points are split between all winning factions based on relative population.

In any cooperative victory, the overall winner receives 1/2 the points of every allied faction's population score.

APPENDIX 1

NOTES AND TIPS

NOTES AND TIPS

GENERAL TIPS

- Pick your faction wisely. The bonuses and penalties intrinsic to each faction may seem minor, but they exert a constant influence on the faction's development throughout the entire game. Therefore, you want to select a faction where the abilities are an asset to your personal style and long-term strategy, rather than a detriment.

- Don't be afraid to use the governors and automate units. This can make gameplay flow much more smoothly, without reducing your actual control over your units and bases in any significant fashion.

- Watch how you place your bases. Try to use all the resources from as many squares as possible. Don't place bases directly within one another's production radius, but it's okay to let the radii overlap a bit. Try not to let any potentially productive squares go to waste.

- Build several colony pods early in the game, to give your faction some territory as quickly as possible. From a strategic perspective, it's never a good idea to have all your eggs in one basket. Plus, more bases gives you bigger energy reserves, faster tech research, and increased capacity to produce Secret Projects and offensive units.

- When you start a base, build a defensive unit right away (more than one, at higher levels of play). Also build at least one former per base.

- Make sure to build several bases on the coast. This allows your faction to produce sea-based units.

- Never forget that units can hide in fungus.

- Explore as much as you can early on, while rival factions are small and relatively friendly and mind worms are young and wimpy.

- Don't mess with your economy settings until drones actually start to become a problem in your bases (and even then, see if you can take care of the problem with social choices or simple facilities first).

- A good basic strategy for building base facilities is simply to build the cheapest ones first. However, you might want to concentrate on network node (particularly if you have an artifact, or expect to build the Virtual World Secret Project) and hab complex (if your population is growing quickly). Do not build pressure domes or punishment spheres unless you know exactly what they're for and are certain they're what you want (see **Appendix 2: Facilities**, p. 163)—these facilities are useful only in specialized circumstances, and the punishment sphere can actually hold you back in specific ways.

- The more Secret Projects you can hog for yourself, the better. Even the ones you don't plan to use are useful, because you're keeping them away from some other faction.

- The earliest Secret Projects are among the most useful, particularly the Human Genome Project and the Virtual World, both of which can give your faction a power edge in stability.

149

- Plant forests to make arid squares productive. Plant some early to give them time to grow.

- If a rival wants to trade technology, trade technology. Every tech advance helps your faction, and an even trade is a good deal—it puts you that much ahead of the other factions not involved in the trade.

- If your faction achieves clear dominance over the other factions, call an election and make yourself Planetary Governor. It's worth it for the trade windfall alone.

- Secrets of the Human Brain can give you an important tech edge in the early part of the game. Unfortunately (for the other factions), the University and the Peacekeepers are about the only factions with a realistic shot at it. All other factions require some major luck to get this tech first (though it can happen).

APPENDIX 2

TABLES

TABLES

TERRAFORMING ENHANCEMENTS

Name (Sea Name)	Prerequisite Technology	Turns to Build	Keystroke
Farm (Kelp Farm)	Centauri Ecology (Doctrine: Flexibility)	4	F
Soil Enricher	Adv. Ecological Engineering	8	F
Mine (Mining Platform)	Centauri Ecology (Doctrine: Flexibility)	8	M
Solar Collector (Tidal Harness)	Centauri Ecology (Doctrine: Flexibility)	6 (4)	S
Forest	Centauri Ecology	4	Shift F
Road	Centauri Ecology	Variable	R
Mag Tube	Monopole Magnets	Variable	R
Bunker	Adv. Military Algorithms	5	K
Airbase	Doctrine: Air Power	10	Shift .
Sensor Array	Centauri Ecology	4	O
Remove Fungus (Sea Fungus)	Centauri Ecology (Doctrine: Flexibility)	6	F
Plant Fungus (Sea Fungus)	Ecological Engineering (Doctrine: Flexibility)	6	Ctrl F
Condenser	Ecological Engineering	12	N

Echelon Mirror	Ecological Engineering	12	Shift E
Thermal Borehole	Ecological Engineering	24	Shift B
Aquifer	Ecological Engineering	18	Q
Terraform UP	Environmental Economics	12	[↑]
Terraform DOWN	Environmental Economics	12	[↓]
Terraform LEVEL	Centauri Ecology	8	Shift -

RESOURCE PRODUCTION TABLES

Underlying Terrain	Nutrients	Minerals	Energy
Raininess			
Arid	0		
Moist	1		
Rainy	2		
Rockiness			
Flat		0	
Rolling		1	
Rocky	0 [1]	1	
Elevation			1-4 [2]
Ocean	1	0	0

153

Fixed Squares

(The production of the following squares is fixed, regardless of underlying terrain.)

Underlying Terrain	Nutrients	Minerals	Energy
Base	2	1	2
Note: bases get resource bonuses as well			
Forest [3]	1	2	0
Monolith	2	2	2
Thermal Borehole	0	6	6
Fungus [4]	0–2	0–2	0–2
Modifiers			
River			+1
Farm	+1		
Kelp Farm	+2		
Soil Enricher	+1		
Condenser	+1 [5]		
Echelon Mirror			+1 [6]
Tidal Harness			+2
Mine	−1 [7]	+1 or 2 [8]	
Road		+1 [9]	
Mining Platform		+1 or 2 [10]	

Underlying Terrain	Nutrients	Minerals	Energy
Nutrient Bonus	+2		
Mineral Bonus		+2	
Energy Bonus			+2
Recycling Tanks [11]	+1	+1	+1

1 Rocky terrain negates all nutrient production from raininess.

2 In order to harvest energy based on a square's elevation, the square must have a solar collector. Squares with solar collectors yield 1 energy for each thousand meters above sea level, starting at 1 for squares 0 to 1,000 meters above sea level, up to 4 for squares over 3,000 meters above sea level.

3 Harvesting a forest square (i.e., building any enhancement other than a road in that square) yields a one-time bonus of 5 minerals. Tree Farm and Hybrid Forest facilities each increase nutrient production in forest squares within that base's production radius.

4 Your ability to extract resources from fungus improves as you acquire new technologies. See Fungus, p. XX.

5 Also raises the raininess by one increment in a two-square radius.

6 Also provides +1 energy to every adjacent square with a solar collector.

7 A mine will not reduce nutrient production to zero.

8 +1 in rolling terrain, +2 in rocky terrain, +3 in rocky with road.

9 Roads provide +1 minerals in rocky squares with a mine (total bonus from road and mine: +3). Roads do not provide a bonus to mines in rolling terrain.

10 Bonus is +1 until the discovery of Advanced Ecological Engineering, +2 thereafter.

11 Recycling tanks only affect the central base square.

155

TERRAIN EFFECTS ON MOVEMENT

Rocky or Forest square
: 2 movement points to enter (however, these squares can always be entered by any unit having at least one full movement point remaining).

Sea fungus square
: 3 movement points to enter (however, these squares can always be entered by any unit having at least one full movement point remaining).

Land fungus square
: Trying to enter a land fungus square (successfully or not) always ends your unit's movement, unless the unit is a mind worm boil, or your faction possesses the Xenoempathy Dome Secret Project.

These penalties have no effect if moving across the square on a road or mag tube.

Road square
: 1/3 movement point.

Magtube square
: no movement point cost to follow a magtube.

River movement
: 1/3 movement point.

Air units.
: Terrain has no effect on the movement of air units.

TERRAIN EFFECTS ON COMBAT

Xenofungus provides concealment (see Flora, p. 39).

Artillery.	+25% attack bonus per level of altitude (see Artillery Combat, p. 100).
Mobile units in smooth or rolling terrain.	+25% attack bonus.
Any unit in rocky terrain.	+50% defensive bonus.
Any unit in xenofungus.	+50% defensive bonus, unless it is being attacked by a native life-form (either human-spawned or "wild") in which case the unit gets no defensive bonus (see next entry).
Any native life-form in xenofungus.	+50% combat bonus

SOCIAL FACTORS

ECONOMY

-3	-2 energy each base
-2	-1 energy each base
-1	-1 energy at HQ base
0	Standard energy rates
1	+1 energy each base
2	+1 energy each square
3	+1 energy each square; +1 commerce
4	+1 energy/sq; +2 energy/base; +2 commerce
5	+1 energy/sq; +4 energy/base; +3 commerce

EFFICIENCY

-4	ECONOMIC PARALYSIS
-3	Murderous inefficiency
-2	Appalling inefficiency
-1	Gross inefficiency
0	High inefficiency
1	Reasonable efficiency
2	Commendable efficiency
3	Exemplary efficiency
4	PARADIGM ECONOMY

 SUPPORT

-4 Each unit costs 2 to support; no free minerals for new base.

-3 Each unit costs 1 to support; no free minerals for new base.

-2 Support 1 unit free per base; no free minerals for new base.

-1 Support 1 unit free per base

0 Support 2 units free per base

1 Support 3 units free per base

2 Support 4 units free per base

3 Support 4 units OR up to base size for free

MORALE

-4 -3 Morale; + modifiers halved

-3 -2 Morale; + modifiers halved

-2 -1 Morale; + modifiers halved

-1 -1 Morale

0 Normal Morale

1 +1 Morale

2 +1 Morale (+2 on defense)

3 +2 Morale (+3 on defense)

4 +3 Morale

159

POLICE

-5   Two extra drones for each military unit away from base

-4   Extra drone for each military unit away from base

-3   Extra drone if more than one military unit away from base

-2   Cannot use military units as police. No nerve stapling.

-1   One police unit allowed. No nerve stapling.

0   Can use one military unit as police

1   Can use up to 2 military units as police

2   Can use up to 3 military units as police

3   3 units as police. Police effect doubled

GROWTH

-3   ZERO POPULATION GROWTH

-2   -20% growth rate

-1   -10% growth rate

0   Normal growth rate

1   +10% growth rate

2   +20% growth rate

3   +30% growth rate

4   +40% growth rate

5   +50% growth rate

6   POPULATION BOOM

PLANET

-3 Wanton ecological disruption; -3 fungus production

-2 Rampant ecological disruption; -2 fungus production

-1 Increased ecological disruption; -1 fungus production

0   Normal ecological tension

1   Ecological safeguards; mind worm capture 25%

2   Ecological harmony; mind worm capture 50%

3   Ecological wisdom; mind worm capture 75%

PROBE TEAMS

-2 -50% cost of enemy probe team actions; enemy success rate increased

-1 -25% cost of enemy probe team actions; enemy success rate increased

0   Normal security measures

1   +1 probe team morale; +50% cost of enemy probe team actions

2   +2 probe team morale; doubles cost of enemy probe team actions

3   +3 probe team morale; bases and units cannot be subverted

161

RESEARCH

-5 Labs research slowed by 50%

-4 Labs research slowed by 40%

-3 Labs research slowed by 30%

-2 Labs research slowed by 20%

-1 Labs research slowed by 10%

0 Normal research rate

1 Labs research speeded by 10%

2 Labs research speeded by 20%

3 Labs research speeded by 30%

4 Labs research speeded by 40%

5 Labs research speeded by 50%

INDUSTRY

-3 Mineral costs increased by 30%

-2 Mineral costs increased by 20%

-1 Mineral costs increased by 10%

0 Normal production rate

1 Mineral costs decreased by 10%

2 Mineral costs decreased by 20%

3 Mineral costs decreased by 30%

4 Mineral costs decreased by 40%

5 Mineral costs decreased by 50%

FACILITIES

Facility	Cost	Maint	Prerequisite Tech	Effect
Aerospace Complex	80	2	Doctrine: Air Power	+2 Morale: Air; Air Def +100%
Bioenhancement Center	100	2	Neural Grafting	+2 Morale: ALL
Biology Lab	60	1	Centauri Empathy	Research and Psi
Centauri Preserve	100	2	Centauri Meditation	Ecology Bonus
Children's Creche	50	1	Ethical Calculus	Growth/Effic/Morale
Command Center	40	Var.	Doctrine: Mobility	+2 Morale:Land
Energy Bank	80	1	Industrial Economics	Economy Bonus; free with Quantum Mach.
Fusion Lab	120	3	Fusion Power	Econ and Labs Bonus
Genejack Factory	100	2	Retroviral Engineering	Minerals; More Drones
Hab Complex	80	2	Industrial Automation	Increase Population Limit
Habitation Dome	160	4	Super Tensile Solids	Increase Population Limit
Headquarters	50	0	None	Efficiency
Hologram Theatre	60	3	Planetary Networks	Psych and Fewer Drones

---

Facility	Cost	Maint	Prerequisite Tech	Effect
Hybrid Forest	240	4	Planetary Economics	Econ/Psych/Forest
Nanohospital	240	4	Homo Superior	Labs and Psych Bonus
Nanoreplicator	320	6	Matter Editation	Minerals Bonus
Naval Yard	80	2	Doctrine: Initiative	+2 Morale:Sea Sea Def +100%
Nessus Mining Station	120	0	Self-Aware Machines	+1 Minerals ALL BASES
Network Node	80	1	Information Networks	Labs Bonus; free with Self-Aware Mach.
Orbital Defense Pod	120	0	Self-Aware Machines	Missile Defense
Orbital Power Transmitter	120	0	Advanced Spaceflight	+1 Energy ALL BASES
Paradise Garden	120	4	Sentient Econometrics	+2 Talents
Perimeter Defense	50	0	Doctrine: Loyalty	Defense +100%
Pressure Dome	80	0	Doctrine: Flexibility	Submersion/Resources
Psi Gate	100	2	Matter Transmission	Teleport
Punishment Sphere	100	2	Adv. Military Algorithms	No Drones/-50% Tech
Quantum Converter	200	5	Quantum Machinery	Minerals Bonus

Facility	Cost	Maint	Prerequisite Tech	Effect
Quantum Lab	240	4	Quantum Power	Econ and Labs Bonus
Recreation Commons	40	1	Social Psych	Fewer Drones; free with Sent. Econometrics
Recycling Tanks	40	0	Biogenetics	Bonus Resources; free with Adv. Ecol. Engin.
Research Hospital	120	3	Gene Splicing	Labs and Psych Bonus
Robotic Assembly Plant	200	4	Industrial Nanorobotics	Minerals Bonus
Skunkworks	60	1	Adv. Subatomic Theory	Prototypes Free
Sky Hydroponics Lab	120	0	Orbital Spaceflight	+1 Nutrient ALL BASES
Stockpile Energy	0	0	None	Minerals to Energy
Tachyon Field	120	2	Probability Mechanics	All Defense +100%
Temple of Planet	200	3	Secrets of Alpha Centauri	Ecology Bonus
Tree Farm	120	3	Environmental Economics	Econ/Psych/Forest

165

Aerospace Complex. Repairs damaged air units quickly. Air units built here receive two morale upgrades. Base must have an Aerospace complex before it can produce space-based facilities

Bioenhancement Center. All military units built here receive two morale upgrades. Any alien life-forms you breed at this base gain a +1 lifecycle bonus.

Biology Lab. +2 research per turn. Any alien life-forms you breed at this base gain a +1 lifecycle bonus.

Centauri Preserve. Reduces effect of industry on Planet's ecology. Any alien life-forms you breed at this base gain a +1 lifecycle bonus.

Children s Creche. Base receives +2 on growth scale and +2 on efficiency scale. All negative morale effects are cancelled for units in base square; instead such units receive a +1 morale modifier. Reduces base's vulnerability to enemy mind control.

Command Center. Repairs damaged ground units quickly. Ground units built here receive two morale upgrades.

Energy Grid. Increases energy reserves at base by 50%.

Fusion Lab. Increases energy reserves at base by 50% and research at base by 50%.

Genejack Factory. Increases minerals output at base by 50%, but also increases the number of drones at base by one and increases vulnerability to enemy mind control. Cumulative with all other facilities of this type.

Hab Complex. Allows population of base to grow beyond size 7.

Habitation Dome. Allows population of base to grow beyond size 14. Base must already have Hab Complex.

Headquarters. Administrative center of your colony. +1 energy. No inefficiency. Enemy probe teams may not attempt mind control here.

Hologram Theatre. Reduces number of drones by two, and increases psych output of base by 50%.

Hybrid Forest. Increases nutrient and energy output of forest squares. Increases psych at base by 50% and energy reserves at base by 50%, and, combined with Tree Farm, eliminates the ecological damage caused by terraforming. Cumulative with Tree Farm.

Nanohospital. Increases psych at base by 25% and research at base by 50% and reduces number of drones by one. Reduces population loss caused by genetic warfare and other disease outbreaks. Cumulative with Research Hospital.

Nanoreplicator. Increases minerals output at base by 50%. Cumulative with all other facilities of this type.

Naval Base. Repairs damaged naval units quickly. Naval units built here receive two morale upgrades.

Nessus Mining Station. Each Nessus Mining Station increases the minerals output of every base by +1. Can only be produced by bases with Aerospace Complexes. Minerals bonus is halved for bases without Aerospace Complexes, and cannot in any event exceed the size of the base.

167

Network Node. Increases research at base by 50%. Base can study alien artifacts.

Orbital Defense Pod. Each undeployed Orbital Defense Pod has a 50% chance to prevent a Planet Buster attack against any of your bases. Defense pods may only deploy once per turn; when no undeployed pods remain, a Planet Buster can only be stopped by sacrificing one of the already-deployed pods.

Orbital Power Transmitter. Each Orbital Power Transmitter increases the energy output of every base by +1. Can only be produced by bases with Aerospace Complexes. Energy bonus is halved for bases without Aerospace Complexes, and cannot in any event exceed the size of the base.

Paradise Dome. Two extra talents at this base.

Perimeter Defense. Increases defense multiplier of base by one. This effectively doubles defense strength (or triples it when combined with a Tachyon Field).

Pressure Dome. Allows base to survive submersion. Also counts as Recycling Tanks for this base.

Psi Gate. Units can teleport between bases containing Psi Gates.

Punishment Sphere. Eliminates both drones and talents at this base, and decreases vulnerability to enemy mind control, but reduces labs output by 1/2.

Quantum Converter. Increases minerals output at base by 50%. Cumulative with all other facilities of this type.

Quantum Lab. Increases energy reserves at base by 50% and labs at base by 50%. Cumulative with Fusion Lab.

Recreation Dome. Reduces number of drones in colony by two.

Recycling Tanks. Increases nutrient, minerals and energy output of base square.

Research Hospital. Increases psych at base by 25% and research at base by 50% and reduces number of drones by one. Reduces population loss caused by genetic warfare and other disease outbreaks.

Robotic Assembly Plant. Increases minerals output at base by 50%. Cumulative with all other facilities of this type.

Skunkworks. Eliminates additional cost to prototype new units at this base.

Sky Hydroponics. Each Sky Hydroponics Lab increases the nutrient output of every base by +1. Can only be produced by bases with Aerospace Complexes. Nutrient increase is halved for bases without Aerospace Complexes, and cannot in any event exceed the size of the base.

Stockpile Energy. All minerals produced at base are immediately converted to energy reserves (each 2 minerals makes 1 energy).

Tachyon Field. Increases defense multiplier of base by one. This is cumulative with Perimeter Defense, for a net tripling of defense strength at base.

Temple of Planet. Reduces effect of industry on Planet's ecology. Any alien life-forms you breed at this base gain a +1 lifecycle bonus. Cumulative with Centauri Preserve.

Tree Farm. Increases psych output at base by 50% and energy reserves at base by 50%. Increases nutrient output in forest squares. Halves the ecological damage caused by terraforming (farms, mines, roads, etc.).

169

SECRET PROJECTS

Secret Project	Cost	Prerequisite Technology	Effect
Ascent to Transcendence	2000	Threshold of Transcendence	End of Human Era
Ascetic Virtues	300	Planetary Economics	Pop. Limit Relaxed; +1 Police
Bulk Matter Transmitter	600	Matter Transmission	+2 Minerals Every Base
Citizens' Defense Force	300	Intellectual Integrity	Perimeter Defense Each Base
Clinical Immortality	500	Matter Editation	Extra Talent Every Base
Cloning Vats	500	Biomachinery	Population Boom At All Bases
Command Nexus	200	Doctrine: Loyalty	Command Center Each Base
Cyborg Factory	400	Mind/Machine Interface	Bioenh. Center Every Base
Dream Twister	400	The Will to Power	Psi Attack +50%
Empath Guild	200	Centauri Empathy	Commlink For Every Faction
Human Genome Project	200	Biogenetics	+1 Talent Each Base
Hunter-Seeker Algorithm	300	Pre-Sentient Algorithms	Immunity to Probe Teams
Living Refinery	400	Advanced Spaceflight	+2 Support (social)
Longevity Vaccine	300	Bio-Engineering	Fewer Drones or More Profits
Maritime Control Center	300	Doctrine: Initiative	Naval Movement +2; Naval Bases
Merchant Exchange	200	Industrial Base	+1 Energy Each Square Here

170

Secret Project	Cost	Prerequisite Technology	Effect
Nano Factory	400	Industrial Nanorobotics	Repair Units; Low Upgrade Costs
Network Backbone	400	Digital Sentience	+1 Lab Per Commerce/Net Node
Neural Amplifier	300	Neural Grafting	Psi Defense +50%
Pholus Mutagen	400	Centauri Genetics	Ecology Bonus; Lifecycle Bonus
Planetary Datalinks	300	Cyberethics	Any Tech Known To 3 Others
Planetary Transit System	300	Industrial Automation	New Bases Begin At Size 3
Self-Aware Colony	500	Self-Aware Machines	Maintenance Halved; Extra Police
Singularity Inductor	600	Controlled Singularity	Quantum Converter Every Base
Space Elevator	500	Super Tensile Solids	Energy +100%/Orbital Cost Halved
Supercollider	300	Applied Relativity	Labs +100% At This Base
Telepathic Matrix	600	Eudaimonia	No More Drone Riots; +2 Probe
Theory of Everything	400	Unified Field Theory	Labs +100% At This Base
Universal Translator	400	Homo Superior	Two Free Techs
Virtual World	300	Planetary Networks	Network Nodes Help Drones
Voice of Planet	600	Threshold of Transcendence	Begins Ascent To Transcendence
Weather Paradigm	200	Centauri Ecology	Terraform Rate +50%
Xenoempathy Dome	300	Centauri Meditation	Fungus Movement Bonus

171

Ascent to Transcendence. Completes the Transcendence sequence and ends the Human Era. The Ascent cannot be started until the Voice of Planet is operational.

Ascetic Virtues. Increases the population limit of your bases by two, and increases your society's tolerance for use of police and military units (+1 Police).

Bulk Matter Transmitter. +2 minerals at every base.

Citizens Defense Force. Counts as a Perimeter Defense at every base.

Clinical Immortality. One extra talent at every base. Doubles your votes in elections for Planetary Governor and Supreme Leader.

Cloning Vats. All of your bases enter a permanent state of Population Boom and will grow every turn provided nutrient output is sufficient and hab facilities are adequate. The negative effects of the power and thought control social engineering choices are eliminated.

Command Nexus. Counts as a Command Center at every one of your bases.

Cyborg Factory. Counts as a Bioenhancement Center at every base.

Dream Twister. +50% to Psi Attack.

Empath Guild. Allows you to contact any leader, and gives you an infiltrator in every faction. You get +50% votes in elections for Planetary Governor and Supreme Leader.

Human Genome Project. One extra talent at every base.

Hunter-Seeker Algorithm. Renders your units and bases completely immune to probe team infiltration of any kind.

Living Refinery. Decreases minerals required to support military units: +2 Support on Social Engineering table.

Longevity Vaccine. Two less drones at every base if your society's economics are planned. One less drone at every base if economics are simple or green. Energy reserves increased by 50% at this base for free market economies.

Maritime Control Center. Increases the movement rate of all naval units by two, and counts as a Naval Yard at every one of your bases.

Merchant Exchange. +1 energy in every square at this base.

Nano Factory. Units can be repaired quickly and completely even when not in base squares. The cost to upgrade units is reduced by 50%.

Network Backbone. +1 research at this base for every point of Commerce this base receives, and +1 research for every Network Node in existence on Alpha Centauri, regardless of the player owning the Network Node. Eliminates the negative effects of Cybernetic Society.

Neural Amplifier. +50% to Psi Defense.

Pholus Mutagen. Reduces effect of industry on Planet's ecology at all of your bases. Additionally, the fungus confers on all of your units the same combat benefits normally reserved for alien life-forms. Any alien life-forms you breed gain a +1 lifecycle bonus.

Planetary Datalinks. You automatically discover any technology discovered by any three other factions.

Planetary Transit System. Any new bases you found begin at population level 3. One less drone at all bases of population level 3 and under.

Self-Aware Colony. Energy maintenance cost for facilities is halved at all of your bases. If use of police is allowed under the current social model, all of your bases are considered to have an extra police unit.

Singularity Inductor. Counts as a Quantum Converter at every base, and reduces the ecological effects of mineral production.

Space Elevator. Doubles energy reserves production at this base, and doubles mineral production rate at all of your bases when producing orbital facilities. Your units equipped with drop pods may now make orbital insertions anywhere on the Planet. All Aerospace Complex restrictions on orbital facilities are waived.

Supercollider. Research output at this base is doubled.

Telepathic Matrix. Drones never riot at your bases. All of your probe teams receive a +2 morale modifier.

Theory of Everything. Research output doubled at this base.

Universal Translator. Two free tech advances on completion. Any number of alien artifacts can be cashed at this base.

Virtual World. In addition to their normal effect, Network Nodes count as Hologram Theatres at each of your bases: reduce number of drones by two and increase psych output of base by 50%.

Voice of Planet. Begins the Ascent to Transcendence sequence. Any faction can now begin the Ascent to Transcendence. Any alien life-forms you breed gain a +1 lifecycle bonus.

Weather Paradigm. Increases terraforming speed by 50% for all tasks except for Remove Fungus. Your formers may build Condensors and Boreholes, and may raise/lower terrain, even if you have not yet discovered the appropriate technologies.

Xenoempathy Dome. All xenofungus squares are treated as roads, and the rate at which your formers remove and/or plant fungus is doubled. Any alien life-forms you breed gain a +1 lifecycle bonus.

UNITS

Speed/Cost. Number of moves per turn, and cost for the base unit.

Domain. Where the unit operates.

Range in turns from base (air units only).

Cargo. Base number of units that can be transported (multiply by reactor rating).

Preq. Technology required.

Names	Speed/Cost	Domain	Range	Cargo	Prerequisite Technology
Infantry	1	Land		1	None
Speeder	2	Land		1	Doctrine: Mobility
Hovertank	3	Land		1	Nanominiaturization
Foil	4	Sea		2	Doctrine: Flexibility
Cruiser	6	Sea		4	Doctrine: Initiative
Needlejet	8	Air	2	1	Doctrine: Air Power
Chopper	8	Air	1	1	Mind/Machine Interface
Gravship	8	Air	0	1	Graviton Theory
Missile	12	Air	1	0	Orbital Spaceflight

175

Chassis	Speed	Modality	Dimensions	Modifiers
Infantry	8km\hr	Manual/tracked	n.a.	+25% when attacking a base
Speeder	102km\hr	Wheeled	7.7x3.6x2.9m	+25% when attacking in open
Hovertank	227 km\hr	Aircushion	6.9x3x3m	+25% when attacking in open
Foil	62 km\hr	Airfoil	162x24.25x17.5m	None
Cruiser	115 km\hr	Naval keel	200x50.5x20m	None
Needlejet	766 km\hr	Fixed-wing aircraft	18.6x12.5x4.4m	None
'Chopper	523 km\hr	Rotary	15.5x6x4m	None
Gravship	1021 km\hr	Graviton booster	22x8x6m	Range unaffected by fuel
Missile	232.5 km\hr	Assisted airflow	15.5x.5x.5m	Destroyed on impact

ARMAMENT

Weapon	Attack Rating/Cost	Mode	Prerequisite Technology
Hand Weapons	1	Projectile	None
Laser	2	Projectile	Applied Physics
Particle Impactor	4	Projectile	Nonlinear Mathematics
Gatling Laser	5	Energy	Superconductor
Missile Launcher	6	Missile	Synthetic Fossil Fuels
Chaos Gun	8	Projectile	Superstring Theory
Fusion Laser	10	Energy	Organic Super Lubricant
Conventional Payload	12	Projectile	Orbital Spaceflight
Tachyon Bolt	12	Energy	Unified Field Theory
Plasma Shard	13	Missile	Advanced Spaceflight
Quantum Laser	16	Energy	Quantum Machinery
Graviton Gun	20	Projectile	Applied Gravitonics
Singularity Laser	24	Energy	Controlled Singularity
Planet Buster	Special	Projectile	Orbital Spaceflight
Psi Attack	-1	Missile	Centauri Psi

PROJECTILE WEAPONS

Weapon	Ammo	Muzzle Vel.	Rate of Fire	Max Range	Target Acq.
Hand Weapons	7.62mm UN standard	2100 fps	120\min (max.)	550 m	Visual
Particle Impactor	10mm caseless Kinetic Energy	2500 fps	1100\min	2700 m	Optical
Plasma Shard	15 mm Mass-energy shell	Var; max 4000 fps	160\min	16 km	Charged particle
Chaos Gun	9mm caseless Field Disruptor	3000 fps	10\min	11 km	Field Differential
Graviton Gun	2mm 3-stage particle-accelerated	9800 fps	2000\min	1.4 km	Nanoremote
Missile Launcher	Mk. 12(t) "Sabre" missile	Mach 2.2	6\min	90 km	IR signature

ENERGY WEAPONS

Weapon	Active Medium	Type	Pulse Duration	Wave-length	Peak Power	Burn Rate (1 steel)
Laser	Diode	Fiber-coupled	5 nsec	193 nm	.84 gw	.76 sec
Gatling Laser	Neodymium-glass	Conductively cooled stacked array	2 nsec	107 nm	.96 gw	.52 sec
Fusion Laser	Neodymium-YAG	Actively cooled stacked array	15 nsec	573 nm	2.4 gw	.14 sec
Tachyon Bolt	Molecular hydrogen	Active liquid coolant	1 usec	680 nm	5 gw	.07 sec
Quantum Laser	Temporal field distortion	Crystal diffusion	n.a.	.005 nm	Var.	n.a.
Singularity Laser	Temporal induction	Singularity boundary	Relative	.001 nm	n.a. (approach inf.)	Relative

OTHER

Psi Attack
Range: Line of sight
Active Medium: Patterned energy
Peak power: Inverse to distance
Type: Compelled dissociative
Target acquisition: Psi lock

Planet Buster
Explosive force: 296 gt TNT
Designation: Mk. 714 Plasma bomb
Target acquistion: Charged particle
Active kill radius: 2000 km

NONCOMBAT PACKAGES

Package	Cost	Prerequisite Technology
Colony Module	10	None
Terraforming Unit	6	Centauri Ecology
Troop Transport	4	Doctrine: Flexibility
Supply Transport	8	Industrial Automation
Probe Team	4	Planetary Networks
Alien Artifact	36	n.a.

DEFENSES

Defense	Defensive Strength	Defends Against	Prerequisite Technology
No Armor	1	Projectile	None
Synthmetal Armor	2	Projectile	Industrial Base
Plasma Steel Armor	3	Both	High Energy Chemistry
Silksteel Armor	4	Energy	Silksteel Alloys
Photon Wall	5	Energy	Photon/Wave Mechanics
Probability Sheath	6	Both	Probability Mechanics

Neutronium Armor	8	Energy	Matter Compression
Antimatter Plate	10	Both	Matter Editation
Stasis Generator	12	Both	Temporal Mechanics
Psi Defense	-1[1]	Both	Eudaimonia

[1] Psi Defense Cost is 6.

Defense	Type	Density	Thickness	Tensile Strength
Synthmetal Armor	Chobham (modified)	2.3 kg\l	250mm	Base
Plasma Steel Armor	Mass-energy composite	2.5 kg\l	520mm	5x base
Silksteel Armor	Bonded	2.5 kg\l	520mm	23x base
Photon Wall	Refractive field	n.a.	2m	46x base
Probability Sheath	Phase adjustment	n.a.	n.a.	97x base
Neutronium Armor	Kinetic diffusion	4kg\l	755mm	198x base
Antimatter Plate	Reactive	-4 kg\l	Var.	560x base
Stasis Generator	Temporal field distortion	n.a.	n.a.	n.a.
Psi Defense	Pattern refraction	n.a.	n.a.	(resistance is proportional to distance)

REACTORS

Reactor	Value/Power	Hit Points		Prerequisite
Fission Plant	1	10		None
Fusion Reactor	2	20		Fusion Power
Quantum Chamber	3	30		Quantum Power
Singularity Engine	4	40		Singularity Mechanics

Reactor	Rating	Throughput	Effic.	Discharge	Fuel Source
Fission Plant	32,700 kw	29,000 kw	89%	52 r	Plutonium
Fusion Reactor	68,000 kw	63,000 kw	93%	67 r	Ionized deuterium
Quantum Chamber	148,000 kw	142,000 kw	97%	21 r	Deuterium-tritium mix
Singularity Engine	>4 mill. kw	Var	Var	n.a.	Vizorium-5

REACTOR DETERMINES

- Unit hit points (10 x Reactor Value)
- Radius of Planet Buster destruction (1 x value square radius)
- Carrying capacity of sea units (foil 2 units x value / cruiser 4 units x value)
- Move bonus to air units with antigrav struts special ability (+2 x value)
- Higher value reactors make complex units cheaper to build

SPECIAL ABILITIES

Ability	Abbrev	Cost	Prereq.	Desc
AAA Tracking	AAA	1	Adv. Military Algorithms	x2 vs. air attacks
Air Superiority	SAM	1	Doctrine: Air Power	Attacks air units
Amphibious Pods	Amphibious	1	Doctrine: Initiative	Attacks from ship
Antigrav Struts	Grav	1	Graviton Theory	+1 movement rate (or +Reactor*2 for Air)
Blink Displacer	Blink	1	Matter Transmission	Bypass base defenses
Carrier Deck	Carrier	1	Nanometallurgy	Mobile Airbase
Clean Reactor	Clean	2	Bio-Engineering	Requires no support
Cloaking Device	Cloaked	1	Frictionless Surfaces	Invisible; Ignores ZOCs
Comm Jammer	ECM	-1	Adv. Subatomic Theory	+50% vs. fast units
Deep Pressure Hull	Sub	1	Nanometallurgy	Operates underwater
Deep Radar		0	Adv. Military Algorithms	Sees 2 spaces
Drop Pods	Drop	2	Mind/Machine Interface	Makes air drops
Empath Song	Empath	2	Centauri Empathy	+50% attack vs. Psi
Fungicide Tanks	Fungicidal	1	Synthetic Fossil Fuels	Clear fungus at double speed

Ability	Abbrev	Cost	Prereq.	Desc
Heavy Artillery	Artillery	-7	Polymorphic Software	Bombards
Heavy Transport	Heavy	1	n.a.	+50% transport capacity
High Morale	Trained	1	Intellectual Integrity	Gains morale upgrade
Hypnotic Trance	Trance	-1	Secrets of the Human Brain	+50% defense vs. PSI
Nerve Gas Pods	X	1	High Energy Chemistry	Can +50% offense (Atrocity)
Non-Lethal Methods	Police	1	Intellectual Integrity	x2 Police powers
Polymorphic Encryption	Secure	1	Pre-Sentient Algorithms	x2 cost to subvert
Repair Bay	Repair	1	Nanometallurgy	Repairs ground units on board
Slow Unit	Slow	0	na.a	-1 moves
Super Former	Super	1	Adv. Ecological Engineering	Terraform rate doubled

TECHNOLOGY TREE

Technology	Abbrev.	Prerequisites	Notes
Adv. Ecological Engineering	EcoEng2	Fusion, EnvEcon	
Advanced Military Algorithms	MilAlg	DocFlex, OptComp	
Advanced Spaceflight	Space	Orbital, SupLube	
Advanced Subatomic Theory	Subat	Chemist, Poly	
Applied Gravitonics	AGrav	Gravity, DigSent	
Applied Physics	Physic	None	
Applied Relativity	E=Mc2	Super, Subat	
Bio-Engineering	BioEng	Gene, Neural	Increases intrinsic defense to gene warfare
Biogenetics	Biogen	None	Increases intrinsic defense to gene warfare
Biomachinery	BioMac	MindMac, Viral	Increases intrinsic defense to gene warfare
Centauri Ecology	Ecology	None	Increases nutrient production in fungus

Technology	Abbrev.	Prerequisites	Notes
Centauri Empathy	CentEmp	Brain, Ecology	
Centauri Genetics	CentGen	CentMed, Viral	Increases minerals production in fungus
Centauri Meditation	CentMed	EcoEng, CentEmp	Increases energy production in fungus
Centauri Psi	CentPsi	CentGen, EcoEng2	Increases nutrient production in fungus
Controlled Singularity	ConSing	SingMec, AGrav	
Cyberethics	Cyber	PlaNets, Integ	
Digital Sentience	DigSent	IndRob, MindMac	Improves Probe Team morale
Doctrine: Air Power	DocAir	Fossil, DocFlex	
Doctrine: Flexibility	DocFlex	Mobile	
Doctrine: Initiative	DocInit	DocFlex, IndAuto	
Doctrine: Loyalty	DocLoy	Mobile, Psych	
Doctrine: Mobility	Mobile	None	
Ecological Engineering	EcoEng	Ecology, Gene	

Technology	Abbrev.	Prerequisites	Notes
Environmental Economics	EnvEcon	IndEcon, EcoEng	Increases commerce income
Ethical Calculus	EthCalc	Psych	
Eudaimonia	Eudaim	SentEco, WillPow	
Frictionless Surfaces	Surface	Unified, IndRob	
Fusion Power	Fusion	Algor, Super	
Gene Splicing	Gene	Biogen, EthCalc	Increases intrinsic defense to gene warfare
Graviton Theory	Gravity	QuanMac, MindMac	
High Energy Chemistry	Chemist	Indust, Physic	
Homo Superior	HomoSup	BioMac, DocInit	
Industrial Automation	IndAuto	IndEcon, PlaNets	Increases commerce income
Industrial Base	Indust	None	
Industrial Economics	IndEcon	Indust	Increases commerce income
Industrial Nanorobotics	IndRob	NanoMin, IndAuto	Increases commerce income
Information Networks	InfNet	None	
Intellectual Integrity	Integ	EthCalc, DocLoy	

Technology	Abbrev.	Prerequisites	Notes
Matter Compression	MatComp	Metal, NanoMin	
Matter Editation	NanEdit	HAL9000, Solids	Increases intrinsic defense to gene warfare
Matter Transmission	Matter	NanEdit, AlphCen	Increases minerals production in fungus
Mind/Machine Interface	MindMac	DocAir, Neural	Improves Probe Team morale
Monopole Magnets	Magnets	String, Alloys	
Nanometallurgy	Metal	ProbMec, DocInit	
Nanominiaturization	NanoMin	Magnets, SupLube	
Neural Grafting	Neural	Brain, IndAuto	
Nonlinear Mathematics	Chaos	Physic, InfNet	
Optical Computers	OptComp	Physic, Poly	
Orbital Spaceflight	Orbital	DocAir, Algor	
Organic Superlubricant	SupLube	Fusion, Fossil	
Photon/Wave Mechanics	DocSec	E=Mc2, Alloys	
Planetary Economics	PlaEcon	EnvEcon, Integ	Increases commerce income

Technology	Abbrev.	Prerequisites	Notes
Planetary Networks	PlaNets	InfNet	Improves Probe Team morale
Polymorphic Software	Poly	Indust, InfNet	Improves Probe Team morale
Pre-Sentient Algorithms	Algor	MilAlg, Cyber	
Probability Mechanics	ProbMec	DocSec, Algor	
Quantum Machinery	QuanMac	Quantum, Metal	
Quantum Power	Quantum	Surface, PlaEcon	
Retroviral Engineering	Viral	BioEng, MilAlg	Increases intrinsic defense to gene warfare; Allows gene warfare atrocity
Secrets of Alpha Centauri	AlphCen	CentPsi, SentEco	"Secrets"; first discoverer gains free tech; Reveals map; Increases energy production in fungus
Secrets of Creation	Create	Unified, WillPow	"Secrets"; first discoverer gains free tech
Secrets of the Human Brain	Brain	Psych, Biogen	"Secrets"; first discoverer gains free tech
Self-Aware Machines	HAL9000	Space, DigSent	Improves Probe Team morale

189

Technology	Abbrev.	Prerequisites	Notes
Sentient Econometrics	SentEco	PlaEcon, DigSent	Increases commerce income
Silksteel Alloys	Alloys	Subat, IndAuto	
Singularity Mechanics	SingMec	Create, HAL9000	
Social Psych	Psych	None	
Super Tensile Solids	Solids	MatComp, Space	
Superconductor	Super	OptComp, Indust	
Superstring Theory	String	Chaos, Cyber	
Synthetic Fossil Fuels	Fossil	Chemist, Gene	
Temporal Mechanics	TempMec	Eudaim, Matter	Increases energy production in fungus
The Will to Power	WillPow	HomoSup, CentPsi	
Threshold of Transcendence	Thresh	Create, TempMec	Increases minerals production in fungus
Transcendent Thought	TranT	Thresh, ConSing	
Unified Field Theory	Unified	Magnets, E=Mc2	

CITIZENS

Citizen	Prerequisite Technology	Made Obsolete By	Bonus to Economy	Bonus to Labs	Bonus to Psych
Doctor	None	Empath	0	0	+2
Drone	None				
Empath	Centauri Meditation	Transcend	+2	0	+2
Engineer	Fusion Power		+3	+2	0
Librarian	Planetary Networks	Thinker	0	+3	0
Talent	None				
Technician	None	Engineer	+3	0	0
Thinker	Mind/Machine Interface	Transcend	0	+3	+1
Transcend	Secrets of Alpha Centauri		+2	+4	+2
Worker	None				

PLANETARY COUNCIL PROPOSALS

Proposal	Prerequisite Technology	Effect
Elect Planetary Governor	None	New Governor Appointed
Global Trade Pact	Planetary Economics	Commerce Rates Doubled
Increase Solar Shade	Advanced Spaceflight	Global Cooling; Sea Levels Drop
Launch Solar Shade	Advanced Spaceflight	Global Cooling; Sea Levels Drop
Melt Polar Caps	Adv. Ecological Engineering	Global Warming; Sea Levels Rise
Reinstate U.N. Charter	Adv. Military Algorithms	Atrocity Prohibitions Return
Repeal Global Trade Pact	Planetary Economics	Commerce Rates Halved
Repeal U.N. Charter	Adv. Military Algorithms	Atrocity Prohibitions Lifted
Salvage Unity Fusion Core	Orbital Spaceflight	+500 Energy Credits Every Faction
Unite Behind Me As Supreme Leader	Homo Superior	Diplomatic Victory; Game Ends

FREE FACILITIES FROM SECRET PROJECTS

Successful completion of certain secret projects provide free facilities at every one of your bases.

Secret Project	Free Facility
Citizen's Defense Force	Perimeter Defense
Command Nexus	Command Center
Cyborg Factory	Bioenhancement Center
Maritime Control Center	Naval Yard
Singularity Inductor	Quantum Converter
Virtual World	Hologram Theatres

APPENDIX 3

OPTION SCREENS

APPENDIX 3. OPTION SCREENS

RIGHT-CLICK (🖱) MENU

🖱 on a square offers a detailed menu of options.

- **Move Cursor to Here.** Moves the cursor to the square on which you 🖱.

- **Move Unit to Here.** Moves the active unit to the square on which you 🖱.

- **Center on Active Units.** Centers the map on your active unit. Can be used if you've lost track of where the next unit to move is.

- **Activate Units Here.** Activates the units on the square on which you 🖱.

- **End the Turn.** Cancels any further actions and ends the turn.

- **Info On This Square.** Displays information about the square in the **Status View** (see p. 25).

- **Help.** Displays **Help Menu** (see p. 31).

In addition, the 🖱 menu may display additional options depending on the contents of the square.

If there is a **base** in the square, the options include:

- **Zoom To Base.** Opens the **Base Control Screen** (see p. 66).

- **Change Production.** Opens the **Production Readout** for the base (see p. 78).

- **Hurry <current project>.** Where <current project> is the name of the project currently underway. See **Build Orders**, p. 67.

- **Set To Explore.**

- **Set to Discover.**

- **Set to Build.**

- Set to Conquer.

  (These four are options for the base governor. See **Governor**, p. 69.)

If the active unit is in the square, the options include:

- Action. Opens the **Action Menu** (see p. 46).

If the active unit is a terraformer and is in the square, the actions include:

- Terraform. Opens the **Terraform Menu** (see p. 46).

GAME RULES

- **Higher Goal: Allow Victory by Transcendence**

- **Total War: Allow Victory by Conquest**

- **Peace in Our Time: Allow Diplomatic Victory**

- **Mine, All Mine: Allow Economic Victory**

- **One For All: Allow Cooperative Victory.** Your pact brothers can help you achieve victory conditions, and share the victory with you.

- **Do Or Die: Don t Restart Eliminated Players.** Normally, if a faction is eliminated (particularly early in the game), the leadership escapes and founds a new base elsewhere on Planet. Under this option, when a faction's gone, it's gone for good.

- **Look First: Flexible Starting Locations.** When you make planetfall, your colony pod waits for you to order it to build your first base, allowing you to reposition the base if you wish.

- **Tech Stagnation: Slower Rate of Research Discoveries.** Technological progress is slowed down across the board.

- **Spoils of War: Steal Tech When Conquer Base.** When you conquer a base of a faction that possesses technology that your faction does not, you may select one technology to steal.

- **Blind Research: Cannot Set Precise Research Goals.** You select broad categories for your researchers to concentrate their efforts, based on the priorities you set between Explore, Discover, Build and Conquer.

- **Intense Rivalry: Opponents More Aggressive.** The other factions are much more willing to fight (and more likely to gang up on you).

- **No *Unity* Survey: World Map Not Visible.** You know nothing of the world other than squares you have actually explored and their immediate vicinity.

- **No *Unity* Scattering: Supply Pods Only at Landing Sites.** There are some *Unity* pods near your first base, but nowhere else.

- **Bell Curve: No Random Events.** Most random events are disabled.

- **Time Warp: Accelerated Start.** You start the game some years after planetfall, with several bases, technologies and enhancements.

- **Iron Man: Save/Restore Restricted To Exit.** Autosaves are disabled except when you actually leave the game—no going back to undo mistakes.

- **Randomize Faction Leader Personalities.** Leaders behave in unpredictable ways.

- **Randomize Faction Leader Social Agendas.** Faction leaders do not adhere to preset social agendas.

GAME PREFERENCES

PREFERENCES

- **Tutorial Messages.** The game displays "pop-up" hints and suggestions.

- **Design Units Automatically.** The game gives you pre-designed units at each appropriate technological advance.

- **Auto-Prune Obsolete Units.** Automatically deletes obsolete, out-of-production units from your production readout. It is recommended that you leave this option on, as your production readout has a finite number of slots for units, and these can fill up very rapidly with obsolete units.

- **Mouse at Edge Scrolls View.** Moving your mouse to the edge of the screen (not the edge of the map) causes the map to scroll in that direction.

- **Autosave Each Turn.** The game creates a new autosave file at the end of each turn. These files are kept in the AUTO subdirectory of your SAVES directory. To load an autosave, 🖲 on AUTO when the load window opens and select the turn you wish to return to. Autosaves are kept for turns 1-10, 20 and 30 prior to the current turn.

- **Pause at End of Turn.** When your turn is completed, the game pauses until you 🖲 on the TURN COMPLETE button.

- **Move Enemy/Neutral Pieces Quickly.** Visible units from enemy or neutral factions move quickly, without full animation.

- **Move Allied Pieces Quickly.** Visible units from allied factions move quickly, without full animation.

WARNING PREFERENCES

This menu is a list of actions or events that can occur at your bases. You may select whether you wish the game to stop when one of these actions or events occurs. If you choose to be warned about a given situation, you are shown a window asking if you wish to zoom to the base where the situation occurred, or ignore it and proceed with your turn. Even if you have these pop-up warnings off, you still get an automated message about the event in your message window (see Data MFD, p. 26).

- Stop for New Facilities Built

- Stop for Non-Combat Units Built

- Stop for Combat Units Built

- Stop for Prototypes Completed

- Stop for Items Built by Governors/Queues

- Stop for Drone Riots

- Stop for End of Drone Riots

- Stop for Golden Age

- Stop for End of Golden Age

- Stop for Nutrient Low

- Stop for Build Orders Out of Date

- Stop for Population Limit Reached

- Stop for Delay in Transcendence

- Stop for Starvation

- Stop for Mineral Shortages

- Stop for Energy Shortages

- Stop for Random Events

ADVANCED PREFERENCES

- **Radio Buttons Select with Single Click.** A single 🖰 both selects and confirms a button function.

- **Click on Unit Always Cancels Orders.** 🖰 on a unit to cancel any current orders.

- **Confirm Odds Before Attacking.** The game displays combat odds whenever you make an attack move, then waits for you to confirm the attack. This allows you to precisely gauge your odds of winning a combat.

- **Pause Whenever Our Forces are Attacked.** Play stops after you are attacked, so you may analyze combat results.

- **Fast Battle Resolution.** Combat animations are speeded up, so the game moves faster.

- **Move Units With Orders Quickly.** Units carrying out preset movement orders are not animated when moving into each square on their route. They quickly "jump" from square to square.

- **Move All Units Quickly.** Units are not shown moving between squares—they just appear in their next position.

- **Don t Center On Units With Orders.** The game does not recenter on units carrying out multi-turn orders.

- **Zoom-To-Base Doesn t Recenter Map.** Allows you to open a base screen when an event occurs, without centering your map on that base.

- **Detailed Main Menus.** Toggles between long, detailed menus, and shorter ones with fewer options.

- **Detailed Right-Click Menus.** Toggles between a long, detailed 🖰 menu, and a shorter one with fewer options.

- **Right-Click Pops Up Menus.** Allows you to toggle the 🖰 menu on or off. When this option is off, if you 🖰, the cursor moves to the indicated location. You can still get to the 🖰 menu by using (Shift)🖰.

AUTOMATION PREFERENCES

- **Air Units Can Return Home When Reach Limit of Fuel Range.** Air units who exhaust their outbound movement automatically return to the nearest base on the next turn. This keeps you from forgetting about an air unit with low fuel.

- **Automated Formers Can Plant Forests.** Formers on "Auto" (see **Terraform Menu**, p. 46) may plant forests.

- **Automated Formers Can Raise/Lower Terrain.** Formers on "Auto" (see **Terraform Menu**, p. 46) may raise or lower terrain.

- **Automated Formers Can Build Condensers, Boreholes, etc. .** Formers on "Auto" (see **Terraform Menu**, p. 46) may build these enhancements.

- **Automated Formers Can Remove Fungus.** Formers on "Auto" (see **Terraform Menu,** p. 46) may remove fungus.

- **Automated Formers Can Build Sensors.** Formers on "Auto" (see **Terraform Menu,** p. 46) may build sensors.

- **Cancel Movement Orders When Spot Units w/ Pact.** Any movement orders are canceled when your unit sees a unit from a faction that is a pact brother.

- **Cancel Movement Orders When Spot Units w/ Treaty.** Any movement orders are canceled when your unit sees a unit from a faction with which you have a treaty.

- **Cancel Movement Orders When Spot Units w/ Truce.** Any movement orders are canceled when your unit sees a unit from a faction with which you have a truce.

- **Cancel Movement Orders When Spot Units w/ Vendetta.** Any movement orders are canceled when your unit sees a unit from a faction against which you have a vendetta.

- **Do Not Cancel for Units of Different Class (land/sea/air).** The above cancel options do not apply if your unit is a land unit and the other is a sea or air unit, and so forth.

- **Wake Passengers When Transport Reaches Land.** If a transport moves adjacent to a land square, the units inside automatically activate for orders.

- **Always Investigate Monolith.** A combat unit investigates a monolith any time it visits a monolith square, without requesting your permission.

AUDIO/VISUAL PREFERENCES

- **Background Music.** Toggles background music.

- **Sound Effects.** Toggles sound effects.

- **Voiceovers (Tech and Facility).** Toggles the voiceover quotes that occur when you discover a new technology or build a facility for the first time.

202

- **Voiceovers Stop When Popup Closed.** Voiceovers fade out quickly when you exit the window announcing the project's completion.

- **Secret Project Movies.** Toggles the movies that play when Secret Projects are completed.

- **Interludes.** Toggles the story interludes.

- **Map Animations.** Toggles map animation.

- **Sliding Window.** Sliding menu windows don't slide, they just pop.

- **Sliding Scrollbars.** Sliding scrollbars don't slide, they just pop.

- **Whole Unit Blinks.** The whole active unit blinks, instead of just its status bar.

MAP DISPLAY PREFERENCES

- **Show Fog of War.** Explored squares outside of your current sensor range are dimmer than squares inside that range.

- **Show Map Grid.** The map grid is visible.

- **Show Base Grid.** A line is visible between your bases' production radii and unexploited terrain.

- **Show Base Names.** Base names are displayed below the base icons.

- **Show Production with Base Names.** Base names and current production orders are displayed below base icons.

- **Show Flattened Terrain.** The map is not contoured to show elevation.

APPENDIX 4

ADVANCED CUSTOMIZATION

ADVANCED CUSTOMIZATION

Alpha Centauri includes a full range of editor functions that allow you to create your own maps or scenarios, alter the basic rules of the game, or just plain cheat yourself silly (in single-player games only, of course). The designers encourage players to become designers themselves, and see what new and unexpected challenges their imaginations can create.

SCENARIO AND EDIT MAP MENU OPTIONS

The Scenario and Edit Map menus provide a number of powerful editing tools. They are not considered part of the game itself, and using them cancels the score of any game you are playing, but are provided for your enjoyment. Using these tools, you can create your own scenarios, with custom maps, rules, objectives and situations. Feel free to play around and create new scenarios for your own use and that of your friends. We don't have the space to document all the features in the scenario and map editors, but here's a few basics to get you started:

- **Activate Scenario Editor** Ctrl K. When you want to edit a particular scenario or map, you must first activate the scenario editor from the Scenario menu. Once you've activated the scenario editor, any game underway no longer keeps track of the score.

- **Edit Map options.** The map editor allows you to build or tweak any map using the options provided. Most are self-explanatory. When placing features, whether terrain or enhancements, remember that first you toggle a particular feature, and then Shift⏎ to place that feature, and Shift⏎ to remove that feature. All Edit Map features are displayed as icon toggles in the central information window when the scenario editor is active.

- **Save early, save often.** The map and scenario editors can cause some program malfunctions because of the nature of these alterations. We suggest you save your work early and often. Have fun!

206

EDITING TEXT FILES

Many basic rules of *Alpha Centauri* are set out in plain text files, which you can modify with any text editor. (These files also let you customize the messages and quotes in the game, to humorous or dramatic effect.) You can, for example, eliminate the extra cost for prototypes (or hike it to 200%), or add an attack bonus for non-artillery units attacking the enemy from a higher elevation, or completely re-arrange the starting abilities of a faction.

Important rules files are *alpha.txt*, and the files for the individual factions; *believe.txt*, *gaians.txt*, *hive.txt*, *morgan.txt*, *peace.text*, *spartans.txt* and *univ.txt*. All the diplomatic language in the game can be found in *script.txt*. These can all be found in the game's root directly on your hard drive.

There's not room to describe all the available options here, but the designers have done their best to make it reasonably easy to modify these files, even for non-programmers. Many sections have an entry that describes the function of that section.

If you feel the urge to tinker, have fun. However, a few rules of caution are in order before you start tweaking the game rules:

207

- **Plain text only.** Never, ever, *ever* save in any other format but plain text. Otherwise formatting characters get in which screw things up. You might not even want to open the file in anything other than a plain text editor, to minimize the chances of unwanted formatting.

- **The changes you make do change the game.** Don't be surprised if a relatively minor alteration turns out to have a major effect on game balance.

- YOU TWEAK AT YOUR OWN RISK. If you somehow manage to break the game through file tweaking, you should uninstall the game and delete any remnant files. Our Tech Support department cannot help you if you have deliberately tweaked the game.

- **Save everything.** Before you start messing with the rules files, put the original files, plus any saved games you want to keep (look for files with the .sav suffix) in a separate directory.

- **Total meltdown.** If you mess around with these files severely enough, the possibility exists that you might break the whole system—computers are surprising that way. So once again, if you start playing around with rules files, it's AT YOUR OWN RISK. FIRAXIS Games and Electronic Arts™ will not be held responsible.

Note. You can create custom text files for use with custom scenarios. Create a directory where you will store your scenario, then place the desired custom text files in the same directory. When you launch the game and load a scenario, the game looks for the text files from the same directory as the scenario first. If it doesn't find them, it looks in the root game directory as normal.

MAP EDITOR COMMANDS

Save Map . . . . Ctrl F5	Place At Cursor . . . Ctrl 🖱 (Shift paints)
Load Map . . . . Ctrl Shift F5	Remove At Cursor . Ctrl 🖱 (Shift paints)
Place Elevations 1	Paint & Editor Only Mode . . Scroll Lock
Place Rocky Squares 2	Change Brush Size 7
Place River Sources 3	Set Climate And World Parameters . . 8
Place Special Resources 4	(Slow) Generate Random Map 9
Place Unity Pods 5	(Fast) Generate Random Map 0
Place Terrain Enhancements 6	Toggle "Editor Only" Mode Ctrl Shift F10

SCENARIO EDITOR COMMANDS

Activate Scenario Editor . . . . . . Ctrl K	View Movies... . . . . Shift F8
Omniscient View . . . . Y	Reset Technology . . . . Ctrl F8
Create Unit... . . . . Shift F1	Reset All Factions . . . . . . Ctrl Shift F8
Edit Unit... . . . . Ctrl Shift F1	Edit Faction Diplomacy . . . . . Shift F9
Technological Breakthrough . . Shift F2	Edit Faction Personality . . . . . Ctrl F9
Edit Technology... . . . . Ctrl F2	Edit Faction Strategy . . . Ctrl Shift F9
Switch Sides/Set View... . . . . . Shift F3	Edit Custom Rules . . . . Shift F10
Set Difficulty Level... . . . . Ctrl Shift F3	Edit Scenario Rules . . . . Shift F11
Set Energy Reserves... . . . . . . Shift F4	Edit Scenario Parameters . . . . Shift F12
Set Mission Year... . . . . Shift F5	Edit Scenario Victory . . . Ctrl Shift F12
Eliminate Faction... . . . . Shift F6	Undo . . . . Alt Bksp
Reload Faction . . . . Ctrl Shift F6	Load Scenario . . . . Ctrl Shift F7
Eliminate Units . . . . Ctrl F6	Save Scenario . . . . Ctrl F7
View Replay... . . . . Shift F7	

208

APPENDIX 5

A NEW SUN

A NEW SUN

As the nearest stellar neighbor of the Sol system, there is a great deal more data that can be collected about Alpha Centauri than can be amassed about more remote stars. So far everything we know about Alpha Centauri suggests that an earthlike world, capable of (at least potentially) supporting human life, is entirely possible — and perhaps likely.

THE CENTAUR

The earliest astronomers identified groups of stars that seemed to fit together, into *constellations* ("stars together"). The most familiar of these include the twelve constellations of the zodiac — the constellations through which the Sun "passes" as the Earth completes its yearly revolution.

About A.D. 135, the Greek astronomer Ptolemy, working in Alexandria, Egypt, catalogued the twelve zodiacal constellations, plus 36 more. One, just barely visible on the southern horizon, he listed as Centaurus, the Centaur. Alexandria, at 31.1° N, is further south than all of Europe and most of North America (everything but parts of Texas and Florida, and most of Mexico) — no one north of that point can see the Centaur. In fact, the two brightest stars of this constellation are too far south for even Ptolemy to have seen in Alexandria.

Since none of the well-connected astronomers of ancient times even knew about these two stars, they never got the individual names that now identify other bright stars (such as Polaris and Sirius). By the mid-1700s, 40 more constellations had been added to the 48 that Ptolemy had originally catalogued, and these 88 spanned the heavens. In 1603, Johann Bayer published a catalogue, not just of constellations, but of all the brightest stars. The most visible star in each constellation became "Alpha," the second-brightest "Beta," and so forth. The brightest star in the Centaur became *Alpha Centauri*. Alpha Centauri is at the Centaur's hip.

Brief Mythological Sidetrip. Other lands also have myths of half-horse, half-human creatures and races, but Centaurs are best known for their role in Greek mythology. They have the body and legs of a horse, with the torso, arms and head of a human. In some myths they are lustful and aggressive; in other tales they are wise and reserved.

BRIGHT STARS

It's obvious to anyone who sees it that Alpha Centauri is bright, but how bright is it? About 130 B.C., Hipparchus divided the visible stars into "magnitudes." He recorded six levels of magnitude, later more precise measurements have determined that each magnitude is about 2.5 times brighter than the next magnitude. He listed 18 first-magnitude stars; four more were added to his list by later astronomers, stars that were too far south for him to see. These four stars are Alpha and Beta Crucis (in the Southern Cross) and Alpha and Beta Centauri.

In fact, Alpha Centauri is the third-brightest star in the sky, behind Sirius (magnitude -1.42) and Canopus (-0.72), with a magnitude of -0.27. It's over three times brighter than the average first-magnitude star. (For the record, it's the tenth-brightest object in the sky, behind the Sun, the Moon, Venus, Mars, Jupiter, Sirius, Mercury, Canopus and Saturn.)

But why is it so bright? The answer seems obvious today, but let's briefly follow the trail of discovery that astronomers followed.

PROPER MOTION

In the early 1700s, Edmund Halley discovered that a few stars (Sirius, Procyon and Arcturus) actually shifted position in the sky. In particular, bright stars seemed to be more likely to move. That made it likelier that bright stars are bright because they are closer to us. (It had already been decided that stars, unlike planets, were too far away to reflect the light of the Sun, because they didn't seem any larger when viewed under magnification. The resulting theory was that stars generated their own light.)

The motion that Halley discovered is called *proper motion*, because it is motion of the star itself, rather than movement of the Earth. Halley couldn't see Alpha Centauri, but other astronomers soon discovered that it, too, has proper motion. In fact, its motion is greater than that of any other bright star. On the other hand, it's not surprising this motion wasn't detected by earlier astronomers — it takes more than 500 years for Alpha Centauri to transit an arc of space as wide as the moon.

However, the proper motions of several very dim stars — including 61 Cygni (fifth magnitude) and Barnard's Star (ninth magnitude) — are greater even than that of Alpha Centauri. Barnard's Star is almost three times as fast as Alpha Centauri. So which is the better predictor of closeness, brightness or proper motion? (Note that a star coming directly at us, or moving directly away from us, would have no detectable proper motion, no matter how close it is.)

DOUBLE STARS

Double stars are pairs of stars that are apparently so close that it's hard to distinguish them individually. Alpha Centauri turns out to be a double star. It wasn't originally thought that double stars were actually close to each other, just that they were on the same line as seen from the Earth. However, when astronomers started listing double stars, there turned out to be far too many for random distribution of this sort. It seemed likely that many of the double stars were actually part of the same system. Double stars that are bound together in one system are called *binary* stars. Alpha Centauri is a binary, containing Alpha Centauri A and Alpha Centauri B.

Observation of a binary system gives us two more indicators to its distance from our own solar system. The farther apart the two stars appear to be from each other, the closer the system is likely to be to us. This likelihood is drawn from the assumption that all binary stars are actually the same distance apart from each other, which is obviously not true. However, it can serve as an indicator, especially when combined with other data.

The second clue is that the more quickly they revolve around each other, the closer they are likely to be to each other. (Mercury, very close to the Sun, revolves around the Sun in 88 days — Earth days, that is. Jupiter takes almost 12 Earth years for the same revolution.)

Alpha Centauri A and B have one of the widest apparent separations and one of the quickest revolutions (80 years) of all binary stars. The evidence mounted that Alpha Centauri is very close to us.

PARALLAX

As telescopes got better and better, it eventually became possible to measure the parallax of closer stars. *Parallax* is a measure of how much an object appears to shift, when the observer shifts position. In the case of stars, the only way to measure perceivable parallax is to observe a star at two times in the year, six months apart from each other, so that the Earth (and the observer) have shifted from one side of the solar system to the other. In the 1830s Thomas Henderson was able to measure Alpha Centauri's parallax. He determined that Alpha Centauri is 4.4 light-years away from us. (Remember that Alpha Centauri is a binary, so sometimes Alpha Centauri A is closer to us, and sometimes Alpha Centauri B is closer.) No star has since been found to be closer.

PROXIMA CENTAURI

Okay, there is one star closer. Sometimes. In 1913, Robert Innes discovered an eleventh-magnitude star very close to the Alpha Centauri system, with high parallax. It is 0.15 light-years (a trillion miles, or more than 13,000 AUs*) from Alpha Centauri A and B, but turns out to be part of the Alpha Centauri system, nonetheless. Its orbit around the other two stars takes hundreds of thousands of years; for now, it is closer to us than either Alpha Centauri A or B, by the same 0.15 light-years. Officially, it is Alpha Centauri C. Unofficially, it is Proxima Centauri. We'll keep calling Alpha Centauri a binary system, because Alpha Centauri C is too far away, and too small, to materially affect the two larger stars.

* *An AU is an* astronomical unit, *the distance from the Earth to the Sun.*

LUMINOSITY

Once we determine the actual distance of a star, several other bits of data fall into place. We can determine how bright the star actually is — its *absolute magnitude* — by comparing its apparent magnitude from Earth and its distance. It turns out that neither Alpha Centauri A nor Alpha Centauri B is among the stars with the greatest absolute magnitude; their apparent brightness relies a great deal on how close they are to us. For the sake of any colonization efforts, that turns out to be a good thing — both stars have habitable zones (which isn't to say that either star has a planet orbiting it, much less one actually within the habitable zone).

MASS

The fact that Alpha Centauri is a binary system gives us a great deal more information about its stars. We know how far away it is, so we can calculate the average distance between Alpha Centauri A and Alpha Centauri B. If we know this average distance and their *period of revolution* (how long it takes them to complete one revolution around each other), we can determine the total mass of the system. If we can measure how much each moves relative to more distant stars, we can calculate which one is more massive, and by how much. And if we know all of this, we can calculate whether their orbit around each other is closer to a circle or to a long, narrow oval.

SOLAR SYSTEM COMPARISONS

So how similar are Alpha Centauri A and Alpha Centauri B to the Sun?

	Sun	Alpha Centauri A	Alpha Centauri B	Alpha Centauri C
Mass	1.00	1.08	0.91	0.12
Luminosity	1.00	1.45	0.45	0.00006
Spectral Class	G2	G2	K5	M5
Surface Temp	1.00	1.00	0.73	0.50
Diameter	1.00	1.09	0.70	0.25

As you can see, the Sun and Alpha Centauri A are very similar to each other. They are both G2 stars, which means that Alpha Centauri A has the same yellow color as the Sun. Alpha Centauri A is larger and brighter, but not by a great deal. Anyone, or anything, comfortable with the Sun would probably be comfortable with Alpha Centauri A.

Alpha Centauri B is smaller and dimmer than the Sun. It is orange, rather than yellow. Alpha Centauri C is a great deal smaller and dimmer than any of the other three, and is red.

HABITABLE PLANETS

There are limits on the radius at which a planet habitable to mankind might orbit a star. The brighter and hotter the star, the farther out a planet must be to be habitable; the dimmer the star, the closer a planet must be. Alpha Centauri C can have no habitable planets – any planet close enough for life-sustaining sunshine would be quickly ripped apart by gravitational forces. Both Alpha Centauri A and B could have habitable planets, if they weren't part of a binary system.

But what effect might the two stars have on each other's habitable planets? As it happens, very little. If a planet were within either star's habitable zone, it would never come close enough to the other star to be materially affected by it – its orbit would be stable. Take a look at the illustration of our solar system, with the Alpha Centauri binary system superimposed on it. Mentally replace the Sun with Alpha Centauri A. Alpha Centauri A's habitable zone does not reach much beyond the orbit of Mars, and any planet that close to Alpha Centauri A is always too far from Alpha Centauri B to be affected by it.

Now mentally replace the Sun with Alpha Centauri B. Since Alpha Centauri B is cooler than the Sun or Alpha Centauri A, its habitable zone is even closer to Alpha Centauri B. Again, Alpha Centauri A would never come close enough to perturb a habitable planet around Alpha Centauri B.

The same can not be said for planets at greater distances from either of the binaries. Neither star can have a planet with the orbital radius of Jupiter,

Saturn, Uranus or Neptune. In fact, once beyond the radius of Mars, the only stable orbits are those that circle *both* stars.

Even if neither star would perturb each other's habitable planets, they would still be clearly visible. From a planet circling Alpha Centauri A, Alpha Centauri B would be a tiny, dazzlingly-bright yellow-orange light in the sky. It will be a tiny dot, but not quite a point, and it would be far brighter than any full moon — easily bright enough to read by. It would light up the night sides of any moons in the sky, as Earth does to the Moon's dark side if you look carefully when the Moon is a crescent. Depending on the geometry at any given time, soon after sunset or before sunrise you night even see "double crescent" moons! Alpha Centauri C would be just barely visible at darkest night as a red naked-eye star from either Alpha Centauri A or B.

PLANETOGRAPHY

Both Alpha Centauri A and B can clearly support habitable planets. We are not currently aware of any planets orbiting either or both of these stars (although recent investigations using the Hubble telescope suggest that a giant planet or a brown dwarf — a very small star — is orbiting Alpha Centauri C). However, let's assume a habitable planet orbits Alpha Centauri A. It should be named Chiron, after the wisest of all the mythological Centaurs, and the tutor of Achilles, Aesculapius and Hercules. However, anyone who lived there for long might simply call it Planet.

EARTH COMPARISONS

Planet is quite a bit more massive than Earth, with a larger radius. While the larger radius reduces the effects of gravity a certain amount, Planet's greater mass still creates a 30% greater gravitational pull — objects are 30% heavier on Planet than on Earth. Planet is a bit farther from Alpha Centauri A than Earth is from the Sun, but Alpha Centauri A is brighter than the Sun, and these differences offset, so that Alpha Centauri A is almost exactly as bright from Planet as the Sun is from Earth.

Planet's days are only about 18 hours, so sleep cycles must be corresponding-ly reduced. Its years are slightly longer than Earth's years., but not enough to make a noticeable difference. The greater difference is Planet's lack of seasons. With only a slight axial tilt, any seasonal differences are minimal.

Neither of Planet's moons exert as much tidal pull as Earth's moon, but when they combine, tides will run slightly higher than on Earth.

Once every 80 years, as Alpha Centauri B reaches perihelion (its closest approach to Alpha Centauri A), it generates enough heat to increase Planet's average temperature by 0.3° C. That doesn't seem like much, but Planet's cli-mactic system might easily amplify this to uncomfortable levels. In fact, any life native to Planet may have evolved cyclic responses to this event.

Planetary constants	Earth	Planet (Chiron)	P/E Ratio
Mass (kg)	5.98×10^{24}	1.10×10^{25}	1.84
Equat. radius (km)	6380	7540	1.18
Dist. from star (km)	1.50×10^{8}	1.60×10^{8}	1.07
Axial tilt (degrees)	23.45	2.00	0.09
Surface area (km^2)	5.10×10^{8}	7.18×10^{8}	1.41
Standard gravity (m/s^2)	9.81	12.85	1.31
Escape velocity (m/s)	11,184	13,947	1.25
Density (kg/m^3)	5519	6150	1.11
Size of sun (degrees)	0.27	0.27	1.02
Year (Earth days)	365	389	1.06
Year (Planet days)	500	532	1.06
Day (hours)	24.00	17.53	0.73
Mountain height (m)	10,626	8112	0.76
Horizon distance (m)	5051	5493	1.09
Ocean tide (sun) (m)	0.12	0.12	0.94
Ocean tide (Nessus) (m)	0.27	0.18	0.67
Ocean tide (Pholus) (m)		0.11	
Ocean tide (all) (m)	0.39	0.41	1.05

Atmosphere

Planetary constants	Earth	Planet (Chiron)	P/E Ratio
Total pressure (Pa)	101,325	176,020	1.74
Nitrogen (Pa)	79,125	160,000	2.02
Oxygen (Pa)	21,228	15,000	0.71
Argon (Pa)	942	1000	1.06
Carbon dioxide (Pa)	30	20	0.67
Nitrogen	78.09%	90.90%	1.16
Oxygen	20.95%	8.52%	0.41
Argon	0.93%	0.57%	0.61
Carbon dioxide	0.03%	0.01%	0.4
Surface density (kg/m^3)	1.22	2.06	1.68
"Flammability" (mmol K/J)	7.17	2.87	0.40
Effective temp. (°K)	253	261	1.03
Greenhouse effect (°K)	+36	+32	0.90
Surface temp. (°K)	288	293	1.01
Surface temp. (°C)	15.4	19.7	1.28
Solar constant (W/m^2)	1383	1750	1.27

ATMOSPHERIC COMPOSITION

The atmosphere consists of 90.9% Nitrogen, 8.5% Oxygen and .01% Carbon Dioxide. The low oxygen content results in fewer forest fires, a higher proportion of anoxic (oxygen-free) environments — encouraging a large anaerobic ecosystem reducing nitrates to break down organic matter — and a plant ecosystem dominated by the need to conserve carbon.

METEOROLOGY AND CLIMATOLOGY

Planet's larger size and gravity result in a significantly higher sea level pressure than Earth's: 1.74 atmospheres (that is, 74% greater air pressure at sea level than on Earth). This brings the partial pressure of Oxygen (15k Pascals) up to acceptable levels, but the high overall pressure combined with such a large quantity of Nitrogen produces deadly Nitrogen narcosis in unprotected humans. Human colonists would have to wear pressure helmets, at the very least.

The temperature bands running along the surface of Planet are the most obvious climactic pattern. As on Earth, solar energy warms the equatorial areas, and the weather cools as you migrate towards the poles. Thus, equatorial regions produce more energy, while the poles tend to have more mineral resources.

The rainfall patterns of Planet depend on the wind currents, which always blow from west to east. Since the wind carries moisture with it from the oceans, rain tends to fall on the west side of mountain ranges. You can see this trend when looking at a big continent – green predominates on the western coast, indicating a great deal of rainy or moist terrain, while the east coast remains dry and barren. Rainfall determines the amount of nutrients that may be collected, so often the west coast of a continent proves a better source of nutrients than the east coast. On flat continents or small islands, no elevations exist to trap the rainfall, and so moisture tends to be more evenly distributed. Also, river valleys usually have a reasonable amount of rain, so a river running through a dry area can be a good base location.

The warm tropical seas of Planet are breeding grounds for hurricanes, which are also encouraged by the high gravity and rapid rotation. The dense nitrogen atmosphere only partly offsets this. The equatorial cloud belts, however, help to regulate the climate by reflecting sunlight.

OCEANOGRAPHY

At over 20% higher insolation than Earth, Planet has very small polar ice caps. The effect of this on the oceanic circulation is profound. Instead of cold oxygen-rich polar water sinking at the poles and being carried in a current along the ocean floor to the equator (as on Earth today), the circulation is driven in reverse, with warm saline oxygen-poor water sinking at the equator and flowing to the poles. As a result, the bottom waters have little oxygen.

SOIL COMPOSITION

Compared to Earth, silicates are much less common in the soils of Planet. As in the tropics on Earth, warm water leaches the silica from clays, leaving a poor alumina-rich soil. (This does not prevent rain forests from growing, but will inhibit agriculture.) The arctic regions have a higher proportion of acidic soils with a high proportion of organic matter (podzols) which is equally hard to farm. The temperate soil zone, which on Earth is favoured with rich aluminosilicate clays, is much narrower on Planet, and the soils are more likely to be sandy or lime-rich. Bogs are also common.

ECOLOGY

Although basically similar to Earth life, in that it is based on carbon compounds in water, the organisms of Planet have evolved a biochemistry very different from Earth. The scarcity of carbon in the environment, and of dioxygen in the soil, has forced plants to try to make do without O2 (oxygen), and to economize on the use of carbon in structural parts and as an energy storage material. They do this by using a biochemical reaction unknown on Earth. Planet's plants seem to have a special enzyme to encourage this reaction, possibly with the aid of sunlight. They use the nitrate obtained this way to store energy as organic nitro-compounds, to reduce carbonates to carbon, and to carry out respiration in anoxic environments.

The prevalence of anoxic (oxygen-free) environments rich in organic material, combined with the presence everywhere on Planet of nitrated compounds, has led to an astonishing variety of underground organisms which live in the absence of oxygen (though they can use oxygen if it is present) and "breathe" nitrate. This ecosystem apparently has symbiotic relations with the plants and with Planet's animal life. Also note that the prevalence of nitrate in the environment has serious repercussions.

Nitrous oxide is present in only small amounts as it combines with ozone in the stratosphere to break down into N_2 and O_2 (which prevents the build-up of an ozone layer).

When plant material is buried, nitro-hydrocarbons have all they need to "burn," so they do so slowly underground, leaving nothing behind until all the reducing material (hydrocarbon) or all the oxidizing material (nitrate) has gone. Nitrate nearly always runs out first, leaving a residue of carbon compounds. Provided this does not come into contact with oxygen, it fossilizes to produce ordinary fossil fuels. Since Planet has been hot and hypoxic for a long time, it should be expected to have all the oil, shale and coal anyone could want, depending on the efficiency of the ecosystem.

221

Regardless of any attempt to wipe out the underground nitrate respirers, all efforts to return carbon to the biosphere would encourage Planet life to proliferate. Conversely, the huge quantities of nitrate in the soil would be heaven to human farmers.

However, water would have to be treated in order to remove the nitrates so that it is safe to drink; otherwise humans would suffer from methhemoglobinemia, or "blue baby syndrome," where the red blood cells are poisoned so they can't take up oxygen. The best way to treat this water is to pass ozone through it to destroy the nitrate.

NATIVE LIFE

XENOFUNGUS

Xenofungus is a hard, crimson mass of tubular shoots ranging in size from about a foot across to microscopic. It grows in huge, heaped tangles capable of covering thousands of square kilometers of land, with a depth ranging anywhere from 2 to over 25 meters. Anything trying to move through a fungal area must either have (a) the raw tonnage required to break through the mass, (b) the ability to move over its top without shredding itself or becoming bogged down in the mass's many cavities, or (c) the firepower simply to blast its way through.

Xenofungus also grows in the oceans. Sea fungus is a bit more diffuse than the land stuff (tending to grow much taller, but not nearly as dense), but is otherwise basically identical.

Most xenofungus blooms are thousands of years old, and geographically stable. On the rare occasions when they do appear, however, they literally appear almost overnight, growing at a rate of up to a meter an hour, sprouting spontaneously over an area that can encompass hundreds of square kilometers.

Chemical analysis of the fungus indicates that it's a rich source of trace elements and rare minerals with a high potential value in energy, nutrient and mineral production. The only barrier to the full exploitation of the fungus as a natural resource is the evolution of technologies to extract its benefits economically.

The fungus seems to exist in a semi-symbiotic relationship with the **mind worms** (see **Mind Worms**, p. XX). Boils are often reported to originate from fungus blooms, particularly when the blooms are somehow damaged. The worms seems to provide the fungus with a natural defense.

One of the more mysterious and controversial aspects of the fungus is its "song." Certain individuals in the immediate proximity of fungal blooms (anywhere from 5 to 200 kilometers, depending on the individual and the size of the bloom) claim to hear a sort of hum or ululation from the fungus. This "music" is not audible to most, and it cannot be recorded. If it exists at all, it may be a resonance created from the same "psychoactive" field that the mind worms employ. Some (particularly among the Gaian faction, which believes implicitly in the "Song of Planet" and has accorded it a mystical significance) claim the song is ethereally beautiful. Others have alleged that prolonged exposure can drive the human brain to distraction, or even madness.

MIND WORMS

The dominant land species on Chiron is the mind worm. From a distance, an individual worm specimen, with an average length of 10cm, hardly seems a threat. Get closer, however, and a human may experience the power of this species. Visions of horrible tortures and frightful deaths assail the mind, straight out of the victim's worst nightmares. This effect multiplies with the number of worms present, each individual adding its own voice to the attack. With sufficient numbers, the victim goes numb with terror, causing spasms, paralysis, and even death as the autonomous nervous system shuts down. This attack is only a precursor to the worm's main goal: to implant freshly hatched larvae inside the host's brain. One gravid worm, if sufficiently agitated, can burrow through a human skull in thirty seconds — less, if the worm finds easy entry through an eye socket or nasal passage. Once inside the brain casing, the worm implants its ravenous larvae, which thrive and grow as they devour the nutrient-rich tissue around them.

223

Adult mind worms live for less than a month (explaining their urgent need to reproduce as quickly as possible), although they can enter a dormant state that lasts for years when they are in contact with the xenofungus. They reproduce sexually, but are hermaphroditic — each mind worm is capable of both impregnating another and of producing larvae itself. In particularly harsh environmental circumstances, a mind worm is even capable of impregnating itself. Genetically, one mind worm is virtually indistinguishable from any other anywhere else on Planet, right down to the chromosomal level.

Giant swarms, or "boils," of these mottled 10cm nightmares occasionally wriggle out of the fungal beds, attacking settlements and their outlying farms and other enhancements. Victims are paralyzed with terror, and then experience an unimaginably excruciating death as the worms burrow into the brain to implant their ravenous larvae. Only the most disciplined security squads can overcome their fear long enough to trigger the flame guns that can keep the worms at bay.

There is one advantage to destroying a mind worm boil (other than the increased feeling of security). When mind worms combine into boils, their metabolisms change. A few begin building concentrated deposits of rare elements, and when a mind worm boil's "life" is cut short (for example, when one is flamed), these deposits can be recovered and converted directly into energy stores. The value of these deposits, and their mode of recovery, lead to their informal name – *planetpearls*. Mind worms that naturally dissipate do not leave the "husks" in which planetpearls are found – they are only recoverable if the boil is "killed."

There are three distinct vectors of the mind worm boils – land, sea and air. The aquatic vector, dubbed *isles of the deep*, appears to form when suboceanic worms come together into a boil. The biochemical processes of the boil itself produce sufficient gas to make the mass buoyant, causing it to rise to the surface. At that point it takes on a life of its own, including apparent independent movement, and even the ability to perceive and pursue particularly attractive food sources (like human vessels and sea colonies). Isles of the deep in shallow coastal waters have been known to spawn land-based boils that break off from the mother mass and proceed on their own cross-country hunts.

The final vector, the air-borne *Locusts of Chiron*, is the strangest. Periodically, a pre-boil mass of mind worms in a xenofungal bloom spontaneously, and for unknown reason, metamorphoses so that they all grow wings, whereupon the worms take off as a boil-swarm. Locusts of Chiron are rare, and "wild" locusts are rarely seen outside of periods of unusual mind worm activity.

There are three current theories regarding the nature of the mind worms' attack. One depends on biochemistry, suggesting that the species produces some pheromone-like atmospheric chemical which induces hallucinations in the human brain. A second, more exotic explanation has also been posited, that the worms manipulate electromagnetic radiation to attack. The third theory is that the mind worms are able to manipulate a totally new form of energy — a purely psychoactive waveform capable of interfacing with, and distorting the thoughts of, all self-aware creatures.

PLANT LIFE

The bulk of the biomass of Planet, however, consists of basically earthlike green vegetation — algae, fungi and small plants, the most complex of which can be compared to a terrestrial palm tree. Over most of Planet, this vegetation takes the form of a savanna-like carpet of grass and moss, with the occasional "vine" or small "bush" relieving the monotony. The sole exception to this rule is the Monsoon Jungle, where anomalous green vegetation can reach a height of several dozen meters. Whatever its size, however, the green biomass provides many useful proteins that can be efficiently processed for use by humans as nutrients.

225

SYMBIOSIS

Despite the most obvious life-forms (xenofungus and mind worms), life on Planet, in general, is neither hostile to humankind nor particularly noteworthy. However, the intricate and sophisticated symbiosis in which nearly every species participates *is* noteworthy. (In fact, no observed species, whether flora, fauna or otherwise, does *not* participate in this symbiotic dance.) It is common on Earth for two, or sometimes even three or four species, to engage in a symbiotic relationship. On Planet, the symbiotic network essentially embraces every native species. This network works together with extreme efficiency and produces very little organic residue — everything is used, then reused. Therefore, contrary to planetologists' expectations, fossil fuels and the like are unknown on Planet.

It is not too great a stretch to suggest that this intricate network has been woven by conscious intent (without attempting to answer the obvious rejoinder, "Whose intent?").

MOONS

Planet has two moons, Nessus and Pholus, also named after Centaurs. The tidal effects of these two moons were briefly discussed earlier. Here are a few more specifics:

	Earth's Moon	Nessus	N/M Ratio	Pholus	P/M Ratio
Mass (kg)	7.35×10^{22}	6.50×10^{21}	0.09	5.20×10^{20}	0.01
Radius (km)	1740	800	0.46	350	0.20
Dist. from planet (km)	3.84×10^{5}	2.00×10^{5}	0.52	1.00×10^{5}	0.26
Surface area (km^2)	3.80×10^{7}	8.04×10^{6}	0.21	1.54×10^{6}	0.04
Mean gravity (m/s^2)	1.62	0.68	0.42	0.28	0.17
Density (kg/m^3)	3342	3031	0.91	2895	0.87
Synodic month (Earth days)	29.5	7.7	0.26	2.7	0.09
Synodic month (local days)	29.5	10.6	ñ	3.7	ñ
Synodic months/local yr	12.4	50.2	ñ	144	ñ
Angular radius (degrees)	0.26	0.23	0.88	0.20	0.77

OTHER PLANETS

Alpha Centauri B has been dubbed "Hercules" by the inhabitants of Planet. As myth would have it, Hercules was, as much by fortune as by intent, a great nemesis of the Centaurs. He slew Nessus (for attempting to violate Deianira), Eurytion (for attempting to force a marriage with Dexamenus' daughter, Mnesimache) and even his former tutor Chiron (by accident, with a poison arrow). Pholus was killed indirectly — by foolishly picking up Hercules' arrow and dropping it on his toe! Since Alpha Centauri B must either have ejected or prevented the formation of other planets in this system, and could in time be responsible for disrupting the remaining planets, the name is appropriate.

Eurytion (named after one of the Centaurs mentioned above) orbits Alpha Centauri A at about half the radius of Planet. Among the planets orbiting the Sun, Mercury bears the closest similarity to it.

	Eurytion	Earth	E/Earth Ratio	Mercury	E/Merc Ratio
Mass (kg)	5.16×10^{23}	5.98×10^{24}	0.09	3.23×10^{23}	1.60
Equat. radius (km)	2820	6380	0.44	2439	1.16
Dist. from star (km)	7.06×10^{10}	1.50×10^{11}	0.47	5.79×10^{10}	1.22
Surface area (km^2)	9.98×10^{7}	5.10×10^{8}	0.20	7.47×10^{7}	1.34
Standard gravity (m/s^2)	4.33	9.81	0.44	3.63	1.19
Escape velocity (m/s)	4940	11,200	0.44	4300	1.15
Density (kg/m^3)	5503	5519	1.00	5420	1.02
Size of sun (angular degrees)	0.62	0.27	2.31	0.70	0.89
Year (Earth days)	113.8	365.3	0.31	88.0	1.29
Surf. temperature (°K)	438	288	ñ	452	ñ
Surf. temperature (°C)	165	15	ñ	179	ñ
Solar constant (W/m^2)	8999	1383	6.51		

SUGGESTED READING

NONFICTION

ALPHA CENTAURI, THE NEAREST STAR *Isaac Asimov*

Lothrop, Lee & Shepard Company, a Division of William Morrow & Comany, Inc., New York, 1976

Published in 1976, by William Morrow & Company (New York), this book is a bit dated but still contains a solid explanation of how we determined Alpha Centauri *is* the nearest star, plus additional details on the nature and structure of this trinary star system. You'll have a hard time finding it in a bookstore; you might have better luck with the juvenile section of your nearest library.

WWW.NASA.GOV

NASA maintains this website, along with useful links to similar sites. Any of the dated aspects of Asimov's book are well addressed at this site. It contains plenty of current statistics and other data, covering much more than just Alpha Centauri (a good place to start might be their search engine, at www.nasa.gov/search/). It also includes an "Ask the Astronomer" question-and-answer forum, plus an archive of previous answers, that can fill you in on just about anything you want to know astronomical (at image.gsfc.nasa.gov/poetry/astro/qanda.html).

PALE BLUE DOT *Carl Sagan; Ann Godoff (editor)*
Random House, 1994, 1995; Ballantine Books, 1997

Sagan's clear vision of humanity's future in space makes this worth reading cover to cover, not to mention the great pictures.

FICTION

Much inspiration for *Alpha Centauri* came from reading classic works of science fiction. For those interested in reading some great books, *Alpha Centauri* Designer Brian Reynolds offers the following suggested reading list.

228

THE JESUS INCIDENT *Frank Herbert*

A speculative and philosophical *tour de force* by my favorite science fiction author. You'll probably have to search used bookstores for this one, but it's well worth it. My favorite science fiction novel ever. A clear inspiration for the story of Planet.

DUNE *Frank Herbert*

Herbert's more famous masterpiece. If you enjoy stories of human factions tearing at each others' throats, you'll love this.

A FIRE UPON THE DEEP *Vernor Vinge*

A far future epic which includes one of the more interesting alien races I've encountered as well as some really original future concepts and a surprise ending which brings it all together. Also includes some pretty hilarious parodies of internet newsgroups.

ANVIL OF STARS *Greg Bear*

What if the universe is filled with alien races sometimes even more sinister and diabolical than humanity at its worst? To what depths of deception and atrocity will a species descend in order to secure its survival?

SLANT *Greg Bear*

A near future earth where information technology has continued to make quantum advances. I find suspension of disbelief very easy with Greg Bear, because his worlds are coherent and his characters' motives are so plausible.

THE MOTE IN GOD S EYE *Larry Niven and Jerry Pournelle*

The best book I've read on the classic "first contact" concept. A really in-depth study of what makes an alien race tick.

THE REAL STORY *Stephen R. Donaldson*

The first in a series of five. Mostly notable for the amount of sleep I lost reading it. Donaldson is the only author I know who can keep me addicted and on the edge of my seat through five straight books.

RED MARS *Kim Stanley Robinson*

The characters can get a little thin, but this is *the* story on terraforming another world. Extremely well-researched. Hard science fiction at its hardest.

THE YEAR S BEST SCIENCE FICTION *Ed. Gardner Dozois*

An annual collection. Extremely well-chosen and well-edited. My favorite source of science fiction short stories. I take one with me on summer vacation.

JOURNEY TO CENTAURI (EXCERPT)

The following is an excerpt from the web-based episodic story, *Journey to Centauri*, that appeared on the *Alpha Centauri* website beginning June 1, 1998, written by Michael Ely. Visit the *Alpha Centauri* website at www.alpha-centauri.com to find out more about humanity's journey to the New World.

"Captain."

Shapes. Shadows, hovering over him. A sense of threat, darkness eclipsing his vision, and the distant sound of warning klaxons. He tried to lift his hands and could not, tried to speak and felt his throat turn to fire. A deep cold pressed down on him, crushing his bones to ice.

"... this one ... hurry!" The voice again.

More movement, seen through layers of frost and glass. I am the Captain, came his next thought, sharp and coherent. I should be first ....

First out of the sleep. Visions returned to him: the long rough cylinder of the ship, floating above the chaos of Earth. The massive cryobays with their rows of sleeping crew, the white-suited cryotechs moving ghostlike among them. His last memory of lying down in glass and feeling the blue tide rise to swallow him, forty years and a moment of darkness ago. Thinking, hoping, that when he woke again, it would be to the sight of Alpha Centauri's primary cresting the rim of a new planet, a new world.

But now ... something was wrong. Someone, unauthorized, moving around the ship. A wave of dizziness washed over him and his vision blurred into a sea of blue, red lights flashing in the distance. He could feel the ship shaking beneath him.

"We move ..."

A shadow passed over him, and then another. Footsteps retreated. He stared up through the curved top of the cryocell, willing himself into the open spaces of the ship, trying to force his fingers to move. His brain signaled alarm but his heart and muscles, held in near stasis, would not respond.

He waited, helpless, while the ship hurled on and the warning klaxons sounded their three beat sequence.

After interminable moments he heard a click and a hiss, and then a storm exploded beneath him.

> Transmission Received,
> U.N.S. Unity Central Processor.
>
> Impact Detected.
> Fusion drive shut down.
> Severe Damage Hydroponics Mods 2, 3; cryobay 7.
>
> Triggering automatic wakeup of core staff per coded instructions.

v v v

Pravin Lal awakened to the hiss of the transparent capsule door breaking its seal and the feel of the ship's foundation shaking beneath him. His heart began to pound and he closed his eyes, breathing deeply, seeking calm.

When his heartbeat slowed he opened his eyes once more. His training had prepared him for this: disorientation, sleep sickness, a deep fatigue that seemed to nest in his bones. He spit the respirator from his mouth and pulled the IVs from his arm, then lifted his hands, placed them on the glass lid above, and pushed.

The cryocell opened. He was alive.

Around him stretched the expanse of Cryobay Two, silent and vast, filled with over a thousand identical glass capsules, each one bathed in a pale blue light, each with tubes and cables snaking down to conduits in the floor. Over a thousand crew, but his eyes immediately, reflexively, turned to the cell at his left. He climbed to his feet and, ignoring the chill, crossed to it.

He looked down through the glass. There, beneath the frost and bluish tint of the cryogel, he could make out her soft brown shape, indistinct, and the darkness of her long hair. Pria. She looked so peaceful, so far away ... he still remembered her gentleness, and their last strong kiss before the cryotechs closed the cell, locking her away from him.

His practiced eyes scanned the small console above her cell. Everything appeared normal; she had survived. His eyes flickered once across the manual release key, and then he saw the red warning lights flashing at the far end of the cryobay. The ship ... he had almost forgotten the danger. He brushed Pria's cell with his fingers one more time and then turned away.

From a metal shelf at the foot of his vacated cell he lifted a folded uniform ... sleek, comfortable, in the sky blue of the mission's Chief of Surgery, with the U.N. seal on the breast and no country-of-origin markings visible. The Captain had lobbied strongly for that.

He slipped into the uniform and flipped on the small computer sewn into the uniform's sleeve. Status report: the Captain would emerge from cryosleep shortly, along with other core officers and some emergency support staff. It appeared that large portions of the ship's hull had been damaged, along with two of the three hydroponics modules. The fusion drive had shut down.

Pravin entered the Returned to Duty code and headed for the command bay. The ship was racing towards Centauri system at tremendous speed, and without the fusion drive there was no way to stop.

> Log Entry Received,
> Pravin Lal, Chief of Surgery.
>
> I have awakened to find the mission in jeopardy. I go now to join my Captain in the command bay, ready to learn what has gone awry.
>
> I pray the integrity of the ship's datacore remains true. It is the last hope of humankind...all of our knowledge digitized for transit to the new world. If Earth has not survived these last 40 years, then our future lies in the heart of this damaged ship.

v v v

The lid to his cryocell hissed open, and Sheng-ji Yang emerged into darkness and immediate danger. From the shadows surrounding his cell peered the narrow deadly eyes of shredder pistols, their barrels leveled directly at him.

Sheng-ji stood calmly, using his hand against the cryocell to steady himself as waves of post-sleep nausea washed over him. *No weakness* ... his eyes flickered in the darkness, marking the position of every enemy. He could not see their faces ... the main lights in this bay appeared to be malfunctioning, or shut down, and he could see only the other cryocells with their soft blue glow, like phosphorescent flowers in a field of darkness.

He willed his muscles to relax with exquisite control. His eyes flickered, just once, across the black metal lockbox on the shelf at the foot of his cryocell. He wouldn't betray his intentions by looking at the box again, but in his mind he carefully reconstructed the exact positioning of the box on the shelf, its exact height from the floor and the position of the softly glowing shape of the digital print lock. The lockbox carried his personal arsenal: his shredder pistol, a submission rod and several sets of organic restraints.

233

"Move away from the cell. Follow the exact path we have laid for you." came a harsh, gravelly voice from a knot of shadows only two cells away. He looked down to see small glowing blue dots on the floor leading away from his cryocell. *Why?*

"On whose orders?" he asked, his throat husky from disuse ... *let the games begin.*

"Do not answer him," came a soft, steely voice from a position, amazingly, even closer than the other, a peculiar dark knot of shadows barely an arm's length away. A chill crossed him, briefly ... that this person dared to crouch so close to him. He read the shadows quickly, making out a silhouette. The shadow ... this person ... waited with catlike alertness, spine taut as a wire. *Who?*

"Do not answer this man," the voice continued. "You are forbidden to speak to him. And, Doctor Yang, do not speak to them. Simply follow the path we have laid out for you."

"Am I to ..."

Suddenly the shadow exploded into motion, and a black serpent crossed the distance to Yang in a heartbeat. Yang felt red hot wires of pain lace his neck, and he fell to his knees, cursing the post-sleep weakness that dulled his reflexes.

Psych-whip, a part of him thought calmly. *They have been in the armory.* And then he smiled as the pain intensified ... he welcomed it, opened himself to it, letting it dance on his nerves and dissolve into his spine. *Pain, awaken me ....*

"We mean you no immediate harm, but I know of your special talents. You must follow my instructions. Do not speak. Crawl along the blue lines."

He looked at the blue dots on the floor, his head still swimming. His eyes flickered up to one corner of the room, a zone of darkness with the vague sense of a metal bulkhead curving. In that darkness he could imagine the bland silvery eye of the security camera staring down at him, but it could not see into the far corner, where the blue dots led.

He felt the muscles tighten along his back. He felt the cool metal floor beneath his hands.

Abruptly, he stood. Electric tension jolted across the room as shredder pistols twitched to follow him. He could smell the uncertainty ... *should we fire?* ... and it had the metallic tang of fear.

He took one slow pace along the blue dots, shuffling as if from fatigue, and then every muscle in his body exploded backward toward his cryocell as a yell from the bottom of his lungs split the darkness. One roll and he reached back over his head to take the black metal lockbox into his hands ... no wasted motion, no wasted time. He had already seen the action in his mind. And then ...

... no turning back, but instead he went up and over his cryocell, the blue light illuminating him for just a moment. A burst of shredder pistol fire crossed the darkness, humming in a cloud all around him, liquefying the glass beneath his feet, and as he leapt he felt the sharp stinging pain of the psyche whip on his back.

A wave of nausea overtook him and instead of fighting it he used it, followed it down, his body spiraling drunkenly into the space behind his cryocell. He could feel the confusion in the room as shadows lurched forward, orders issued in hisses. No shouts and no further fire ... *near perfect silence*, he thought. *Amazing discipline, as if ....*

No matter. He had moments, and moments were all he needed. Crouched in the darkness he punched the release code into his lockbox. He flexed his hands, deadly weapons in their own right, serpents awaiting their venom.

The box would not open. It remained inert, a block of dead cold metal in his hands. He turned it quickly face up, tried to make out the letters printed on top. "A. Shaw." They had switched lockboxes on him.

A shadowy form rose above him, and he caught a sliver of blue light across familiar features.

"You ..." he said, wanting to buy time.

A dark metal shape crashed into him, and his vision burst into blue fireworks on a night black sky.

235

From the Unity Library,

Doctor Yang's Collection:

> Weapons are the tools of fear;
> a decent man will avoid them
> except in direst necessity
> and, if compelled, will use them
> only with the utmost restraint.
>
> He enters a battle gravely,
> with sorrow and with great compassion,
> as if he were attending a funeral.
>
> Tao Te Ching,
> Steven Mitchell trans.

DESIGNER'S NOTES

Although this is our second product as a company, *Alpha Centauri* has been around, in some form or another, right from the humble beginnings of FIRAX-IS Games. Its story has in many ways paralleled the story of our company — FIRAXIS and *Alpha Centauri* grew together, both changing and evolving over two and a half years. Both faced significant setbacks and periods of self-doubt, but in the end FIRAXIS came together as a company, and as you have hopefully discovered, *Alpha Centauri* came together as one of our best games ever.

In July 1996, the brand new FIRAXIS Games (at the time we were calling it "FIRAXIS Software") consisted of four or five people huddled in some borrowed office space in the back of the Absolute Quality building in Hunt Valley, MD. AQ, a professional game testing company, was also a brand new startup, so times were exciting, to say the least. Yes, the rumors are true: we did in fact buy AQ a phone system and bartered it for their spare office space.

CEO Jeff Briggs worked the phones to rustle up some funding and did all the hard work of actually putting a new company together. Sid Meier and Brian Reynolds worked to scrape together some playable prototype code, and Jason Coleman wrote the first lines of JACKAL, the engine which these days pretty much holds everything together. Office Manager Susan Brookins found us some office furniture and bought crates of Coke, Sprite and Dr. Pepper to stash in a mini-fridge Brian had saved from his college days. We remembered that at some indeterminate point in the past we were considered world class game designers, but our day-to-day lives weren't providing us a lot of positive reinforcement on that point. So for the first nine months of our existence as a company, we clunked over the railroad tracks in the morning, played *Spy Hunter* in the upstairs kitchen, and declared "work at home" days when AQ had competitors in the office.

1996, you may recall, was also the "Year Of The Real Time Strategy Game." Giants strode the industry and remade it in their image. Indeed, our first offering as a company, *Sid Meier's Gettysburg*, is enthusiastically real time, and if you like real time games at all and haven't tried it yet you owe it to yourself to go and find a copy – Sid considers it one of the two best games he's ever designed, and the rest of us are inclined to agree. But we were also convinced that in spite of the industry's headlong rush to get on the real time bandwagon, a strong market still existed for turn-based strategy games. Gamers wanted a new, sweeping epic of a turn-based game, and they wanted us to design it.

At that time, science fiction games were definitely not the first thing that came to mind when you thought about our team. We were known for history-based games. We knew a lot about history and historical games and pretty much left the science fiction and fantasy to everyone else. But we'd just done an epic game based on all of human history up to present times and needed a fresh topic, so at some point someone said "well, how about a future history" – human history from the near to the distant future. Kind of a way to bring our strength with historical games to bear on a science fiction game.

From the beginning, *Alpha Centauri* set out to capture the whole sweep of humanity's future. Not just technology and futuristic warfare, but social and economic development, the future of the human condition, spirituality and philosophy. One challenge we quickly discovered is that whereas most people are at least roughly familiar with the major events of human history, and can easily relate to archetypes like "fire," "nomadic hordes" and "the wheel," they haven't got the foggiest notion of what "Polymorphic Software" might be, since we just made the name up five minutes ago. It takes a lot of work to weave a tapestry of future history which both coheres and makes the future accessible to players.

Since it is, after all, the future we're talking about, we've tried to be extraordinarily flexible in allowing many different possible strategies and different kinds of victory. Whereas we can, for instance, look back on the past and say "well obviously that system of government worked and that one didn't," it's a lot harder to make cogent predictions about future society. We don't even know *what* future governments will be like, let alone whether or not they will work. So in our Social Engineering section we've tried to challenge players to imagine the future for themselves — to create their own future utopias and try them out against other competing visions. Thence also came the idea of "factions," rival groups to challenge players with opposing and contrasting ideologies.

Thrown into this mix are the uniquely science fiction elements of exploring and terraforming an alien world. Since we were trying to create a plausible future history, trans-lightspeed galactic travel seemed a bit unrealistic. We chose instead to start with a near future situation which with only a little extra optimism could actually happen — a human mission to colonize the solar system of our sun's nearest neighbor. It seemed likewise implausible that upon arriving in the Alpha Centauri system humans would discover a thriving community of five or six intelligent quasi-humanoid alien races, so we stuck with human factions to provide rivals and opponents. But alien ecologies and mysterious intelligences are cool, so we've incorporated them into the game as external "natural forces" which serves as a flywheel for much of our back-story and a catalyst for many player actions.

With *Gettysburg* taking up most of our time, we spent *Alpha Centauri*'s first year working up a prototype of basic ideas. Artist Mike Bazzell provided enough preliminary art to get us going, senior programmer Jason Coleman perfected our system code, and lead designer Brian Reynolds hacked a game and some AI together. Sid had a spare fractal algorithm he wasn't going to need for *Gettysburg*, so Brian took it up to Canada for vacation and finished the world generator on the shores of the St. Lawrence. We were playing "games" of *Alpha Centauri* by fall of '96, and by the following summer we were working on the multiplayer engine. We invited veteran game designer Doug Kaufman, with whom we've often worked, to join us as a game balancer and become "the first man on Alpha Centauri." You'll find Doug's ideas well represented throughout the game (the disengage rule, long range bombardment, and energy loans, to name just a few), and he's the guy you can thank when you try some bizarre new strategy and lo-and-behold the game understands it.

Around this time we also began doing some research on the scientific realities involved in interstellar travel. A few tentative posts on the Internet later, we made the acquaintance of Derek "Del" Cotter, a British fan who proved so helpful in setting us straight on astronomy, biology and interstellar travel that we sent him a contract and hired him to do some research. Del provided the technical design for our starship, the U.N.S. *Unity*; designed planets and solar system consistent with current knowledge of the Alpha Centauri system; figured out Planet's vital statistics; and fleshed out our biosphere. Del's interstellar travel research was particularly useful for our web story, which Mike Ely wrote and which appeared in installments on our website during the final months of development. Del even provided some biochemical theories about how the fungus and mind worms might work and generally made it possible for us to do a near future space colonization game without sounding like idiots.

Now skip ahead to late 1997. *Alpha Centauri* was still plodding along, but the schedule was starting to slip and most who played it at the time agreed that it lacked that certain *je ne sais quoi* which makes a game stand out as a classic. Enter Bing Gordon, an industry veteran who co-founded Electronic Arts way back when your humble game designer was just starting high school (you mean he's one of the guys who brought out *Archon*?! Cool!) and who lately serves as its Chief Creative Officer. A long time fan of, um, that other game we wrote, he was excited about working with us on our new project. He saw in *Alpha Centauri* a masterpiece struggling to get out. Bing helped us figure out what was needed to make this the cool thing we all knew it could be. In addition to the fact that we didn't throw the whole game out the window in disgust, you can thank Bing for the Planetary Council and all the extra time we spent making the diplomacy cool. Bing also convinced us to take multiplayer seriously as a *design* challenge as well as a technical hurdle.

A few months before the 1998 E3, the gaming industry's biggest trade show, it was time to get our marketing plan up to speed. Lindsay Riehl, our one-woman marketing department, quickly got this under control, kept the press interested in our progress, and generally helped spread the good news. It was Lindsay who talked us into including Explore/Discover/Build/Conquer in the game as well as the ad campaign, so that what began as a cool marketing tie-in ended up becoming a way to refocus our "Governor" automation (which had previously been intended mainly for advanced players) as a useful learning tool for beginners. Later, Lindsay arranged to fly out EA's marketing team for several days of hands-on play, in a devious, underhanded and ultimately completely successful ploy to hook them on the game and remake them as *Alpha Centauri* evangelists. Many thanks to Alex Carloss, Chris Plummer, Matt Orlich, Audrey Meehan and David Swofford for all the hard work they've put in, and most especially for taking the time to come out and really get to know us and our product.

Alpha Centauri showed well at E3, so it was time to buckle down and get this bad boy finished. How Jason "90-hour week" Coleman and Artist Dave "I'm very afraid" Inscore made it through the summer and autumn of '98 is anybody's guess, but in the end they proved to us that a Sid Meier game can have an interface as polished and integrated as anything in the industry. Producer Tim Train took on the near impossible task of keeping track of what everyone was doing and making a (gasp) schedule, meanwhile coordinating the game manual and foreign language translations and moonlighting as co-designer. On top of all that Tim somehow found time to become our office *Alpha Centauri* champion and provide innumerable good pointers on game tactics for us to include in the AI. When a computer player amasses an overwhelming force and *then* moves up to attack your bases, think of Tim.

Art Director Michael Haire developed some concept sketches for our faction leaders, and Jerome Atherholt painted those beautiful portraits which brought them to life as individuals. Believe me there were a lot of people hovering around his office door the day he was working on Deirdre (by the way, that's pronounced "DEE druh." Got it? Now say it again ten times). He also dug up and/or manufactured all of those dossier photos, and most importantly took on the scary task of designing the final look of Planet itself, drawing all of our terrain, solar collectors, boreholes and so forth. We discovered that everyone had a strong (and different) opinion on what Planet ought to look like (More red! Less red! More detail! Less detail!), and finally one day Executive Producer Jeff Briggs threw us all out and said "Okay, go home. This weekend *Jerome* is going to draw the terrain, and when he's done you can all *look* at it." You done good, Jerome.

Mike Bazzell, in addition to doing pretty much all of our prototype art and having by far the scariest office at FIRAXIS, built all of those cool vehicles and vehicle parts. Imagine being told you have to design a laser cannon that looks just as cool on a hovertank as on a needlejet or a cruiser, or carried around by some infantry guys. And everything has to fit together interchangeably. And rotate! And move in 3-D! But after years of playing with little "sprite guys," it sure is great to watch those needlejets make bank turns. Mike is also responsible for all of our on-screen animations, explosions and so forth.

Meanwhile, Mike Ely directed our Secret Project movies, coming up with a coherent vision, doing storyboards, figuring out which movies needed licensed footage and which we should develop in-house, and working with the artists to bring Planet to life cinematically. Mike made all of the "footage" movies himself, and edited together the final cuts of all the movies. For the 3-D movies, Nick Rusko-Berger was our principal movie man, creating our Opening and Transcendence sequences as well as many of the Secret Projects, such as the Bulk Matter Transmitter. But many of our other artists were heavily involved in movie making as well – Greg Foertsch's movies included the Space Elevator and Hunter-Seeker Algorithm; Dave Inscore created the Command Nexus and Maritime Control Center; and Jerome Atherholt painted the backgrounds for the Citizens' Defense Force.

Music for our movies was composed by Jeff Briggs, our versatile CEO, Executive Producer, Designer and Composer. Dave "Mr. Sound Guy" Evans, our digital sound wizard and mandolin maestro, masterminded our in-game music and did pretty much everything else that involves sound and sound effects. Dave wrote what we suspect may be the first true interactive midi/pcm engine ever to ship with a computer game. He had the fun of going to a sound workshop where everyone was talking about interactive midi as something "a few years down the road" and thinking "heh heh, I've already *done* that." Dave also came up with some literally unspeakable technology to let us support true voice-to-voice transmissions during multiplayer games. Meanwhile, Mike Ely went through unending grueling casting sessions to find us seven faction leaders with good voices, acting skills, *and* authentic accents. Want to make Mike wince? Just sing a few bars of the "Deirdre's got a Network Node" song.

Much still remained to be polished. Art Director Michael Haire designed the faction icons and created individual icons for each of our many technologies, facilities and secret projects. Michael also did many of our scoring screens, as well as prototyping much of our interface. Greg Foertsch created our "monument" reward screen, and did much of our situational payoff art. And while all this was going on, a college senior and mathematics major walked into his career counselor's office and said that what he really wanted to do with his life was "work for a company called FIRAXIS Games." And that's how Chris Pine came to FIRAXIS. Chris did all the report screens on the HQ Menu, and we have to say we had no idea how cool report screens could be until Chris joined us. Now if he'd just give up this "Go" business and learn to play Chess like a normal Firaxian!

With *Alpha Centauri* pulling into the home stretch, Jeff Morris, our Quality Assurance Director, kicked into high gear. Somehow Jeff managed to coordinate testing between three different groups plus FIRAXIS itself, keep our networks running, and still find time to write our install program. Our old sister company, Absolute Quality, with whom we shared office space for so long, handled the on-site testing, and we must say that Dan Schlueter and his team did an excellent job finding the serious problems in our software. Dan, along with colleagues Jim Smith, Ted Paulsen, Graham Boyanich, Ray Lofton and Charles Brubaker, stayed on top of things and helped us get the multiplayer code stable in record time. Origin also contributed Rhea Shelley's test team, which did a most thorough job of combing through the software for the things that are so easy to miss. Thanks!

We'd also like to thank profusely the 25 hardy volunteers who participated in our public beta test. Particularly considering that their only pay consisted of buggy early versions of the game, their enthusiasm and participation was outstanding. We'd never done a public beta test before, but let me tell you we're sold on the idea now, since doing one gave us a perspective on our product we could never have obtained in any other way. Among many other useful suggestions, our beta testers insisted that we add Diplomatic and Economic victories, and yes, even the dreaded Random Events. Thanks to everyone who participated — you really made a difference.

Two and a half years is a long time to work on a project, and many changes have taken place in that time. Amanda Rusko-Berger, Coulby Riehl and Caleb Reynolds were all born during the project. Susan Brookins, who kept us fed and paid and made sure the Gatorade man filled up our machine every week, is now Susan Meier (yes, *that* Meier). The FIRAXIS staff has grown to a whopping 17, and we've got a pretty good view now from the top floor of the Executive Plaza building in Hunt Valley. We're a better team, a happier team, and definitely a wiser team than we were when we started the project. The nest is going to seem a little empty with *Alpha Centauri* gone, but fortunately we've got two outstanding ideas in the works, and maybe even a few after that, so it looks like we'll stay busy for quite a while.

Before we close, we'd like to stop and briefly reflect on the deeper message that *Alpha Centauri* hopes to convey. In the closing years of the twentieth century, humanity stands capable of technological achievements which were never possible in any previous era and which as far as we know may never have been available to any sentient species, ever. The time of miracles is indeed upon us, and yet the nuclear trigger remains armed, population growth continues to overwhelm available resources, our climate shows early signs of running amok, and sooner or later a near-Earth asteroid will probably wipe civilization or even humanity itself from the face of the planet. As a basket in which to keep all our eggs, Earth is more precarious than ever, yet we continue to dilly and dally and just this week Time magazine ran an article calling the International Space Station "a white elephant" that is not worth the money.

Are we content to stew in our collective juices, to turn inward as our planet runs inexorably out of resources and wait for the Universe (or perhaps our next-door neighbors) to grow tired of us and wipe us out? Or shall we claim the planets and stars, distribute our eggs among many baskets, ensure the long-term survival of our species, and in the process embark on the greatest adventure of all time? Mars could be reached within our own lifetimes: manned exploration missions, even colonies, all for a minute fraction of what we spend every year building weapons. The planets lie nearly within reach of current technology, and even a trip to Alpha Centauri is easier than you probably think. Consider Planet's final imperative at the Ascent to Transcendence: bright children of the stars. We can probably eventually do even that if we put our minds to It — what a thought! The stars are waiting for us; we have only to decide that it's worth the effort to go there. Look at the stars on a cold, clear, winter night and think about that. If *Alpha Centauri* inspires a few young scientists and astronauts; if it convinces a few more citizens to write to their congressmen and work to rejuvenate our space program, humanity's space program, that will surely be its greatest and most lasting accomplishment.

And so to end our valedictory, we'd like to thank Sid for all his sage advice; Jeff Briggs for thinking that starting a little company called FIRAXIS might actually be a good idea; Jill Reynolds, Holly Coleman, Yvette Bazzell and all the other FIRAXIS wives and families for enduring 80-hour weeks for longer than anyone should have to endure them; our publisher for bearing with us; and all the others, too numerous to name individually, for working to help make this game great. Thank you, thank you very much. Most of all, we'd like to thank all of our fans, who in the end make all of this possible. As always, we hope you enjoy playing *Alpha Centauri* as much as we enjoyed creating it. Walk with Planet!

Brian Reynolds

Hunt Valley, MD

November 23, 1998

CREDITS/KEY COMMANDS

CREDITS

Created By .Brian Reynolds

With . . . . .Sid Meier, Timothy Train,
Douglas Kaufman, Bing Gordon

And . . . . .Members of FIRAXIS Games

Executive Producer . . . . .Jeffery L. Briggs

Producer . . . . .Timothy Train

System/Interface Programming . . . .Jason Coleman

Sound Engineering/Programming . . . .David Evans

Additional Programming . . .Chris Pine, Jeff Morris

Art Director . . . . . . .Michael Haire (Icons, Scoring)

Graphic Artists Jerome Atherholt (Portraits, Terrain),
Michael Bazzell (3-D Units, Prototyping),
Gregory Foertsch (Payoffs, Movies),
David Inscore (Interface, Planetscapes),
Nicholas Rusko-Berger (Movies, Opening)

Movies and Voices Directed by . . . . . .Michael Ely

Featuring the Voices Of:

Lady Deirdre Skye . . . . .Carolyn Dahl

Chairman Sheng-Ji Yang . . . . .Lu Yu

Academician Prokhor Zakharov . .Yuri Nesteroff

CEO Nwabudike Morgan . . . . .Regi Davis

Colonel Corazon Santiago . . . . . . .Wanda Nino

Sister Miriam Godwinson . . . .Gretchen Weigel

Commissioner Pravin Lal . . . . . . .Hesh Gordon

Planet . . . . .Alena Kanka

Datalinks, Male . . . . .Robert Levy

Datalinks, Female . . . . . . .Katherine Ferguson

Background Music . .David Evans, Jeffery L. Briggs

Movie Music . . . . .Jeffery L. Briggs

Director Of Marketing . . . . .Lindsay Riehl

Master Of Miscellaneous . . . . .Susan Meier

Webmaster . . . . .Michael Ely

Astronomy, Physics & Biology Research Derek Cotter

Intern Coordinator . . . . .Deborah Briggs

Interns . . . . . . .Alex Luskin (Sound Engineering)
Kurt Kotula (Graphic Art), Matt Pierce (Marketing)

Stock Footage Courtesy Of . . .Archive Films, Corbis,
The Image Bank, WPA Film Library

"The Dancing Baby" is used with the permission of
Kinetix, a division of Autodesk, inc.

With Special Thanks To Jill, Ro and Caleb Reynolds

Published By . . . . .Electronic Arts

ELECTRONIC ARTS

EA Godfather . . . . .Bing Gordon

EA Executive Producer . . . . .Andy Hollis

EA Producer . . . . .Bryan Walker

VP Marketing . . . . .Alex Carloss

Director Of Marketing . . . . .Chris Plummer

Product Manager . . . . .Matt Orlich

European Product Manager . . . .Audrey Meehan

Media Relations Manager . . . . .David Swofford

EA Quality Assurance: . . . . .Benjamin Crick,
Daniel Hiatt, Michael Jung, Etienne
Grunenwald, Anatol Somerville, Bobby Joe

QUALITY ASSURANCE

Quality Assurance Director Jeff Morris, FIRAXIS Games

Absolute Quality, Inc. Dan Schlueter, AQ Lead Tester
Graham Boyanich, Charles Brubaker,
Ray Lofton, Ted Paulsen, Jim Smith

Origin Systems, Inc.:
Rhea "Shalom" Shelley, OSI Project Leader
Todd "Balls" Raffray, OSI Assistant Project Leader,
Tim "Quasimodo" Bell, Brett "Beaker" Bonner,
Stacy "Skyline" Davidson, Zafer "Z-man" Hamza,
Kent "Hand" Raffray, Jon "Punchy" Shelus,
Stephen "Money Shot" VanWambeck